READER'S DIGEST

THE POWER OF PLANTS

OTS

ANNATTO is a large shrub, whose prickly pods hold red seeds. These produce an orange-yellow dye, used as a food colouring. In the Amazon, local people make body paints from the seeds and use the leaves to treat upset stomachs and fevers.

At least 40 000 plant species grow in the world's largest river basin, where a single hectare may contain 100 types of tree. Plants from the region include mahogany, kapok, Brazil nut, rubber trees and many with medicinal uses.

HELICONIA 'flowers' are actually bracts (modified leaves) with the true flowers hidden inside. Their vibrant shades of red, orange and yellow attract hummingbirds, which pollinate the plants as they move from flower to flower.

THE GIANT WATER LILY is most at home in slow-flowing sections of the Amazon, where its enormous circular leaves, up to 2.5 m across, can dominate a waterway. Its large, fragrant flowers last only a couple of days, turning from white to deep pink before withering.

PLANT HOTSPO

Plants grow all over the planet, but in some regions the richness and diversity of species is particularly intense. In tropical zones, with long hours of daylight and a warm, humid climate, plants naturally flourish and this is seen in the lush vegetation of tropical rain forests. Elsewhere, unique climatic and geographical conditions have led to thriving plant communities. These hotspots have hundreds or even thousands of species that are 'endemic' – found nowhere else in the world. They are of immense value to botanists, their biodiversity representing a vast genetic resource which we are only just beginning to quantify and appreciate.

THE POTATO PLANT originated in the high Andes, probably near Lake Titicaca. Nearly 4000 varieties are still grown in the region, including many unusual and colourful ones, such as this variety with purple leaves.

CINCHONA is the source of the anti-malarial drug quinine. The trees carry the active compound in their bark, which Andean peoples have harvested for centuries. There are about 40 species, all native to the eastern slopes of the Andes.

1 TROPICAL ANDES

A diverse range of Andean habitats includes subtropical moist broadleaf forests, lush evergreen cloud forests (right) and sparse grasslands, called *puna* and *páramo*, at altitudes above 3500 m. Such diversity of habitats has led to a diversity of plants with 30 000 species recorded. Of these at least half are found nowhere else.

THE GIANT PUYA or *Puya raimondii* grows in the Peruvian and Bolivian Andes at altitudes of around 4000 m. The largest member of the bromeliad family, the giant puya takes up to 150 years to flower and produces the tallest flower spike in the world – some 10 m tall.

OVER MILLIONS OF
RESPONDED AND
DIFFERENT HABITATS,
BREATHTAKING
PLANTS DISPLAY AN
OF POWERS – FROM
ABILITY TO CAPTURE
TO A KNACK FOR
SERVICES OF OTHER

CAPE HEATHS are low-growing shrubs from the same family as heather. They are the most abundant plants in the Cape region, which has more than 600 species of them – the rest of the world has 26.

RHODODENDRONS flourish in the Hengduan Mountains, some growing 20 m tall. Most modern cultivated varieties were bred from specimens first brought from Central Asia to Britain in the 19th century.

3 THE CAPE

South Africa's Cape Floral Region has some of the greatest plant diversity and density in the world. More than 9000 species grow in 80 000 km² of Mediterranean-style dry scrubland, 70 per cent of them known only there. Most are fynbos (Afrikaans for 'fine bush') – evergreen shrubs with hard leaves.

THE ANGR is one of more identified on M uniquely long r spurs, and its s partner is a ha an equally long

4

3

4 MADAGAS

When Madagascar separated from some 160 million years ago, its wi off on a unique evolutionary journ it is home to thousands of plants nowhere else. Vegetation ranges f tropical rain forest to a spiny fore succulent plants in the south (b

GLADIOLI abound in the Cape region along with other wild bulbs, including freesias and agapanthus. Numerous cultivated varieties have been bred from these wild ancestors and are now grown all over the world.

BAOBAB trees tower above the surrounding vegetation. They are a good example of Madagascar's botanical diversity. There are eight baobab species in the world – Madagascar has seven, six of which are endemic to the island.

A region of deep valleys and towering peaks naturally encompasses a variety of topography and climate. Habitats include temperate broadleaf and coniferous forests (above), meadows, wetlands and bamboo forests. Of some 12 000 plant species, about a quarter are endemic.

5 HENGDUAN MOUNTAINS

BAMBOOS form a dense understorey beneath mixed temperate forest trees. These are slender – as opposed to giant – bamboo species and they provide food for the rare red panda that lives in the region.

RAFFLESIA flowers are more than 1 m wide. The plant is a stem parasite and when not flowering on the forest floor, it spreads unseen within the wandering stems of a host vine.

...ECUM ORCHID
...n 1000 orchids
...gascar. It has
...ar-holding
... pollinating
...moth with
...gue.

...CAR

...frica
...fe set
... Today,
...t exist
...n
...of
...ow).

Borneo has 15 000 plant species, and more are still being discovered. Around a third are found nowhere else. Among the island's plants are rare and exotic orchid species, along with the carnivorous giant pitcher plant, which grows on Mount Kinabalu, and the foul-smelling titan arum.

6 BORNEO

SLIPPER ORCHIDS in Borneo include *Paphiopedilum sanderianum* from the rain forests of Sarawak. It grows from the side of limestone cliffs where its ribbon-like petals – up to 1 m long – can dangle freely.

YEARS, PLANTS HAVE ADAPTED TO COUNTLESS

RESULTING IN TODAY'S DIVERSITY OF SPECIES.

ASTONISHING RANGE THE ALL-IMPORTANT ENERGY FROM SUNLIGHT HARNESSING THE LIFE FORMS.

THE
POWER OF
PLANTS

1 PLANT PLANET

2 STRATEGIES FOR LIFE

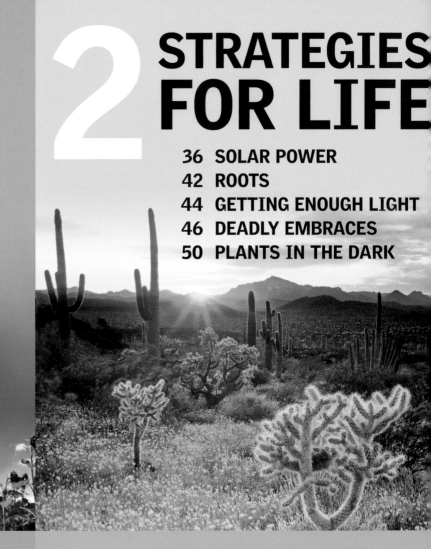

5 THE NEXT GENERATION

6 ARMED RESPONSE

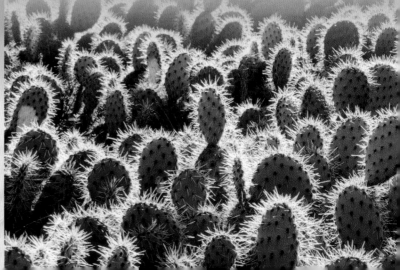

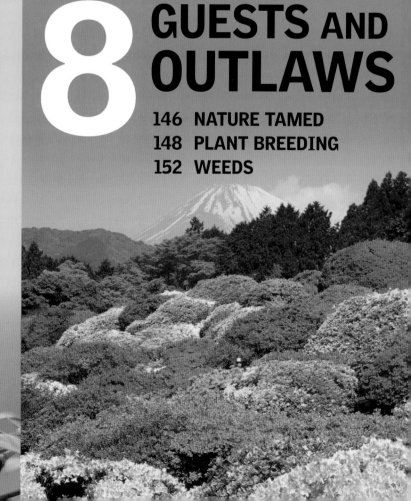

INTRODUCTION

THERE ARE VERY FEW PLACES ON EARTH WITHOUT PLANTS OF SOME KIND. From the parched soils of deserts to the icy tundra of far northern latitudes, the power of plants can be seen in their ability to adapt to just about every habitat. In deserts, many withstand long periods of drought by storing water in their tissues, while at the tops of mountains specialist alpines keep a low profile to avoid harsh ice-laden winds. In swampy regions, a few plants have special snorkel-like adaptations, which poke out of the mud, enabling the roots to obtain oxygen in waterlogged soil. Some plants grow fully submerged in freshwater, others in shallow, well-lit waters off the coast, forming submarine meadows brimming with wildlife.

Earth is often called the 'blue planet' because of its abundance of water, but on land **green** predominates. The green pigment in plants is the **chlorophyll** inside their leaves. It is this that enables plants to capture the energy from sunlight and, through **photosynthesis**, to convert it into chemical energy, which is stored in their tissues. The power of plants to do this makes them the basis of the **food chain**, sustaining most life on Earth. As well as storing energy, plants draw up and capture **minerals** from the soil via their roots, incorporating them

into their tissues as essential nutrients. Plants also absorb **carbon dioxide** and release **oxygen**, and so help to maintain the air that we breathe.

Plants may not be able to move as animals do, but they react to their **environment** in remarkable and proactive ways. They know up from down and sense **light**, growing towards it. They know when the seasons change and time their **reproductive lives** with great precision. They are also skilled at employing the services of other life forms – enticing bees, for example, to carry **pollen** from flower to flower in return for a drink of nectar. Over millions of years, some have evolved very particular **relationships**, such as the partnership between the fig and the **fig wasp**, neither of which can survive without the other.

The result of such adaptations is the huge **diversity of plants**. Some are favoured by humans, such as the many **food crops** we have domesticated and selectively bred. Others, the weeds, remain outlaws – tough survivors that continue to engage farmers in an age-old war of attrition. Plants provide **materials** for construction and **fibres** for textiles; they yield rubber, dyes, oils, resins and medicines. In both gardens and the wild, they also display the **power to delight** with their sheer grace and beauty. What would life be like without the sweet scents and vibrant colours of flowers?

PLANT
PLANET

1

SINCE PLANTS FIRST CAME ONTO LAND, SOME 475 MILLION YEARS AGO, THEY HAVE NOT LOOKED BACK. From tentative beginnings, they have evolved into all shapes and sizes, from spongy mosses to spiny cacti to the mighty redwoods. Plants have colonised every habitat, from lush tropical rain forest to the most inhospitable desert regions; some have even returned to the sea. The ability of plants to adapt to their surroundings and seize any opportunity to grow has been the key to their success, and indeed to ours – without them animal life could not exist. Here we see the great roots of a rain-forest stalwart, the strangler fig, spreading over the ruins of Angkor Wat in Cambodia. It is a salient reminder of the power of plants. The civilisation that built Angkor Wat is now long gone, but the plants remain, and they are reclaiming the site.

CORNERSTONE OF LIFE

DESERT BLOOMS The island of Socotra is home to some weird and wonderful plants, including desert roses, which store water in their swollen trunks.

WE DEPEND ON PLANTS FOR OUR SURVIVAL. NOT ONLY ARE THEY THE FOOD THAT POWERS THE ENTIRE ANIMAL KINGDOM, but as a by-product of feeding themselves plants produce the oxygen we breathe. Plants give us materials such as wood, cotton, hemp and bamboo; they have medicinal applications; their essential oils provide fragrances; and their ancient remains are exploited by us as fossil fuels.

There are around 300 000 species of wild plants worldwide, and their spread into diverse habitats has taken place over millions of years. Some plants can withstand burning sunshine, while others require deep shade. Tropical plants need year-round warmth, whereas trees in Siberia can tolerate temperatures that plummet below -50°C – cold enough to freeze human skin.

Exposed to sizzling hot days, freezing cold nights and little rainfall, desert plants typically show intriguing adaptations. One of the most bizarre-looking desert plants is the Socotran desert rose, a succulent that grows on the island of Socotra in the Arabian Sea, and also known as the sack-of-potatoes plant on account of its bulging stem. From April to October, the tree, which can grow to 3 m tall, endures day after day of hot, dry winds from Africa; thereafter rainfall averages 15 cm and is patchy, and in some years there is none at all. To survive the drought conditions, the plant takes up water when it can and stores it in its stem, which is full of watery tissue and covered in a thick, waxy cuticle.

Plants living at high altitudes, meanwhile, must cope with a very variable climate. There may be hot, dry days in summer and extremes of cold and snow in winter, with exposure to high

ALPINE SURVIVORS When in bloom, the normally greyish vegetable sheep stud the rocky slopes with hummocks of vibrant colour.

levels of ultraviolet light and high winds presenting further challenges. One group of high-altitude specialists are the vegetable sheep, their compact, cushion-like, woolly mounds dotting the mountain ranges of New Zealand. Their tightly packed leaves are covered in a thick coat of silvery white hairs, which serve both to reduce water loss and keep them warm, while deep roots anchor the plants securely to the rock face. Beneath the surface of the mound, which can be up to 1 m across, old leaves rot down and act as a moisture store.

Competition and diversity

In the tropics, light, warmth and moisture may be in plentiful supply but plants growing here face a different problem – competition. Plants that thrive here are the ones that can outdo their neighbours. As a result of this competition, rain forests are among the most species-rich of habitats, with thousands of plant species already identified and many more still remaining to be discovered. It has been estimated that there are around 100 species of large trees occupying just one hectare of forest. Also jostling for position are climbers, epiphytes (rootless plants that perch on tree branches), ferns, palms and mosses. Among the wealth of flowers, the exotic blooms of the heliconias stand out in vibrant shades of red, yellow, orange and pink.

TOTALLY TROPICAL Heliconias put out striking flowers all year round. They grow in humid regions, usually below 450 m.

GREEN INHERITANCE

IT IS HARD TO IMAGINE A WORLD WITHOUT PLANTS, but around 480 million years ago all land was barren rock; there were no fields, no meadows, no forests. Neither was there much in the way of soil – just weathered-out sands, gravels and clays mixed with volcanic ash. The only life on land consisted of occasional patches of lichen and algae that clung to rocks around the shoreline.

In the oceans, it was a different story. Here plant life flourished as the water carried nutrients, physically supported the organisms and facilitated reproduction, carrying sperm to egg through the water and dispersing any offspring. In order to survive on land, plants would need to develop strategies to prevent them drying out and to ensure that reproduction could successfully take place in a less watery environment.

Plant pioneers

The first plants to venture onto land could survive only where there was a surface film of water; they were not so much terrestrial as amphibious, living in damp, humid places. In the absence of stems, leaves or specialised tissue for transporting water and nutrients, their size was limited and they crept over the ground in low-growing mats, never more than about 2 cm high. Instead of roots they anchored themselves to the ground with cells called rhizoids.

These early colonisers were relatives of today's liverworts, hornworts and mosses, known collectively as bryophytes.

Conquering land

About 420 million years ago, plants began to develop specialised tissues to transport water and nutrients. This vascular system, a little like our veins and arteries, included an outer skin, or cuticle, that reduced water loss, thus preventing the plant from drying out. It was perforated with pores, called stomata, to allow the uptake of gases. Since water and nutrients could now be carried to where they were needed, plants could grow larger. The vascular structure also lent physical support, enabling plants to stand upright.

One of the earliest vascular plants known from the fossil record is *Rhynia*. Although, like its predecessors, it had no roots or leaves and held on to the ground with rhizoids, it could spread along the ground by means of a horizontal stem, from which grew branched, upright stems. Some of these were tipped with a tulip-shaped, spore-bearing structure, called a sporangium.

Also among the earliest vascular plants were the ferns, which today are found in a wide range of habitats from moist, shady forests to dry crevices in rock faces. Perhaps the most successful of all the ferns is bracken (*Pteridium aquilinum*), which grows on every continent except Antarctica. Like many other

*DINOSAUR FOOD Tree ferns on Réunion
Island in the Indian Ocean look just like
their prehistoric ancestors.*

*FOSSIL RECORD A horsetail fossil (near
right) shows that the plant (far right) has
changed little since the Carboniferous era,
around 360–290 million years ago.*

ferns, bracken can spread via underground stems (rhizomes) or
by dispersing its spores on the wind, often over great distances.

The horsetails, represented today by the sole genus
Equisetum, also flourished. These primitive-looking plants have tiny
scale-like leaves and sometimes spindly branches, which emerge
from joints, or nodes, along the upright, hollow stems. Spores are
released from cones at the tips of the stems. Horsetails also spread
vegetatively, proliferating by underground rhizomes. The stems
contain silica deposits and were once used to scrub pots and pans,
giving the horsetails their alternative name of scouring rushes.

As the vascular plants thrived and diversified in the
swampy, tropical conditions of the time, they began to spread over
the Earth, covering great swathes of the barren, rocky land with a
carpet of green. The age of land plants had truly begun.

REACHING FOR THE SKY

THE FIRST UPRIGHT PLANTS, SUCH AS *RHYNIA*, WERE JUST ANKLE-HIGH. Yet competition for sunlight, which plants need in order to feed themselves by means of photosynthesis (see page 36), drove them to push upwards. Over millions of years they grew ever taller, until by around 300 million years ago some plants had reached enormous sizes. While giant tree ferns and horsetails grew to heights of up to 10 m, the kings of the early forests were the giant clubmosses, towering 40 m high.

These prehistoric giants had tall, naked trunks perforated by air channels. Meanwhile, a layer of a bark-like cortex around the outside of the stem – an early form of secondary thickening – helped to keep the clubmosses upright. To provide a stable foundation in their swampy habitat, the clubmosses were massively splayed at the base. A system of horizontal, prop-like structures up to 1 m thick, called rhizophores, from which sprouted a raft of root-like structures, anchored the plants in the soil. The trees were topped with a crown of branches carrying simple, strap-shaped leaves, measuring up to 40 cm long. Because they did not develop large crowns, giant clubmosses could grow much closer together than today's forest trees.

Confined to a damp place

Like *Rhynia* before them, the ancient tree ferns, horsetails and clubmosses were all restricted to swampy habitats by a phase of their reproductive cycle. These plants all produced spores – tiny, ready-to-germinate particles launched into the air and dispersed to new wetland sites on the wind. Once there, these particles did not develop into further spore-bearing individuals. Instead, they grew into a sexual generation of the plant, often much smaller, called a gametophyte. These plants produced male and female sex cells, which needed water to make contact. Swimming through their watery habitat, the male sex cells fertilised nearby female cells, which grew into the next spore-bearing generation of the plant for the cycle to begin anew.

Yet even as far back as 385 million years ago, one forest-dweller had already developed an innovation that would pave the way for fully terrestrial plants. *Archaeopteris*,

ANCIENT ORIGINS *The ginkgo's leaf-vein pattern reflects the tree's primitive vascular system.*

ADVANCE GUARD *Despite the name, clubmosses are not mosses but one of the most ancient groups of vascular plants. Today's clubmosses are tiny in comparison with the giants that populated prehistoric forests.*

which grew to a height of 20 m, combined a woody trunk with the fronds of a fern. It, too, reproduced by spores and, like some of the other plants, it produced male and female spores. But there was a subtle difference – its female spores were much larger than its male spores, because they carried a food supply to feed the embryonic plants that would develop from them. Scientists believe that *Archaeopteris* may represent an interim phase between the spore-bearing and seed-bearing plants.

Rise of the seed-bearers

The development of seeds proved a turning point in plant evolution. The first seed-bearing plants were cycads, ginkgos and conifers, collectively known as gymnosperms (or 'open-seed' plants because their seeds are not encased in a fruit). The tough seed coat allowed the seed to remain dormant until conditions were right for germination. And the supply of food inside the seed meant the embryo could tap into a ready supply of nutrients to get it off to a flying start, regardless of where it landed. At first, the gymnosperms were small and crowded out by the giant spore-bearing plants, but the innovation of a seed meant that they could spread into drier regions where the spore-bearers could not go. Also, fertilisation was wind-powered – it did not rely on a watery film. The male cones released pollen that drifted through the air until it reached a female cone, where fertilisation could take place – a mechanism much better suited to a dry, terrestrial environment.

Another major factor that favoured seed-bearing plants was a gradual drying-out of the climate over millions of years as the continents shifted position. By the end of the Carboniferous period, around 290 million years ago, the Earth's swamps had reduced in size and number, limiting the watery conditions the spore-bearing plants needed in order to reproduce. The seed-bearing plants now held sway.

Today, the conifers remain a successful plant group, with huge coniferous forests covering around a tenth of the land surface of the Earth. Around 250 species of cycad, the most primitive living gymnosperm, are known to exist today, while the once enormous family of ginkgos has only one remaining representative, *Ginkgo biloba*, or the maidenhair tree, which grows wild in China and has changed little since dinosaurs roamed the Earth.

The wood from the trees

Besides producing seeds, the gymnosperms had a second advantage over the spore-bearers – they could lay down secondary tissue, better known as wood. This strengthened their stems, enabling them to grow thicker as they grew taller. The thickening trunks could support large, branching canopies that captured available sunlight, enabling the trees to outcompete their shorter neighbours.

At the start of its life, as a seedling, a tree contains in its stem a basic vascular system of water-carrying tubes (xylem) and nutrient-carrying tubes (phloem) arranged in a ring. As the tree grows, it begins to lay down secondary tissue via a layer of actively dividing cells, called the cambium, close to the surface of the trunk. Sapwood, which develops on the inner wall of the cambium, strengthens the tree as well as helping to conduct water up the trunk from the roots. As the layer of sapwood builds over time and the girth of the tree increases, the growth closest to the centre dies and is filled with resins. Waste products from the tree's active cells are dumped in this dark, strong heartwood, which no longer transports water but still provides a central support, although old trees can go on living with their heartwood hollowed out.

A felled tree from a temperate forest will reveal its growth pattern as a series of rings. The rings show the yearly additions of sapwood during spring and summer, followed by a

DOMINANT TREE Mist shrouds the canopy of a dipterocarp rain forest in Borneo. The dipterocarps, which can reach heights of up to 70 m, yield valuable timber, aromatic oils and resins.

ANATOMY OF A TREE A treetrunk is made up of several layers. At the centre is the heartwood – old, dead xylem that acts mostly as a support. Enclosing the heartwood is the sapwood, a layer of newer, living wood containing xylem vessels for transporting water. Next is the cambium, the tissue responsible for laying down both the xylem-filled sapwood in the layer beneath and the sugar-carrying phloem that forms the next layer. While water travels only upwards, sugars and starches move up and down the trunk and branches (see right). Finally, the cork cambium produces the protective crust of bark.

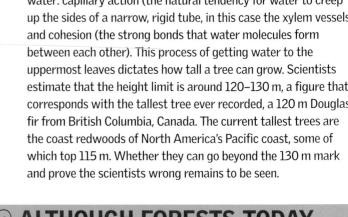

SUGARS AND STARCHES TRAVEL UP AND DOWN THE PHLOEM

WATER TRAVELS UPWARDS IN THE XYLEM VESSELS

XYLEM   CAMBIUM   PHLOEM   CORK CAMBIUM

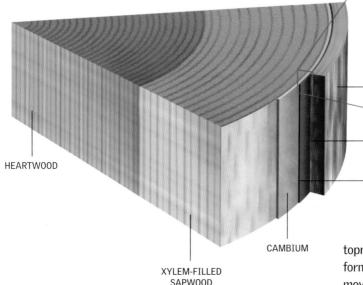

HEARTWOOD

XYLEM-FILLED SAPWOOD

CAMBIUM

BARK

CORK CAMBIUM

PHLOEM

period of dormancy in winter. Since each ring represents one year's growth, it is possible to estimate a tree's age by counting the rings. Their width varies, depending on rainfall and climate. A narrow ring shows that a tree endured a year of drought, while a wide ring indicates a year of plentiful rainfall.

Cells laid down on the outer side of the vascular cambium become secondary phloem tissue for transporting sugars up and down the plant. Next to this is the cork cambium, which produces the outer cork layer, or bark. This may be several layers thick and is essentially a covering of dead, protective cells. The colour, texture and pattern of bark varies with different tree species, from the soft, papery bark of silver birch to the hard, fissured bark of pine. Besides forming a protective barrier to the living cells beneath, bark contains pores, allowing the exchange of gases in and out of the tree.

Water movement

With their remarkable structural engineering, trees can continue to grow for hundreds, sometimes even thousands, of years. The bristlecone pines of North America, for example, are estimated to be up to 4600 years old. There is, nonetheless, a limit to how tall trees can grow. The environment in which a tree grows plays a part in restricting height, as does a tree's genetic make-up – a general limitation on size is programmed into each species' DNA.

The single biggest check to untrammelled vertical growth is the way water is transported up the tree. The xylem vessels in the sapwood that carry water to the topmost leafy canopy are made of hollow cells laid end to end, forming continuous tubes from the roots to the leaves. The water moves up the plant by a process known as transpiration – as water evaporates from the surface of the leaves, more is drawn up behind it. The transpirational pull is helped by two properties of water: capillary action (the natural tendency for water to creep up the sides of a narrow, rigid tube, in this case the xylem vessels); and cohesion (the strong bonds that water molecules form between each other). This process of getting water to the uppermost leaves dictates how tall a tree can grow. Scientists estimate that the height limit is around 120–130 m, a figure that corresponds with the tallest tree ever recorded, a 120 m Douglas fir from British Columbia, Canada. The current tallest trees are the coast redwoods of North America's Pacific coast, some of which top 115 m. Whether they can go beyond the 130 m mark and prove the scientists wrong remains to be seen.

FACTS

ALTHOUGH FORESTS TODAY COVER AROUND 30 PER CENT OF EARTH'S LAND AREA, HALF THE WORLD'S ORIGINAL FORESTS HAVE DISAPPEARED.

98 PER CENT OF THE WATER THAT ENTERS a tree's roots is lost through evaporation, the remaining 2 per cent is used in photosynthesis.

THE CONES OF SOME CYCADS can grow up to 1 m long and weigh 43 kg.

FACTS

THE STATELY REDWOODS

THAT GROW ALONG THE PACIFIC COAST OF
Northern California are the tallest living things on
Earth, regularly reaching a height of over 100 m. In a
forest kept cool and damp in summer by fogs that
sweep in from the sea and where the annual rainfall
is 150–350 cm, these giants live long and well.
Some redwoods survive for 2000 years and reach
a girth of over 7 m.

Redwoods are named after the colour of their
bark and wood. The bark can be 30 cm thick and
helps to protect the tree against the fires that
occasionally sweep through the forest. The wood and
bark are rich in tannins, which impart resistance to
fungal disease and insects.

Some of the largest redwood specimens are
distinguished by names such as Stratosphere Giant,
Icarus, Helios and the Mendocino Tree. Incredibly,
the roots of these giants may only penetrate some
2 m below ground. They do not have a taproot,
but rather a shallow network of branching roots
that can extend as far as 100 m from the trunk.
Hyperion is currently the tallest coast redwood at
115.5 m, although the title-holder changes from time
to time as dead wood falls off the crowns and new
trees are discovered.

CLASS: Pinopsida
ORDER: Pinales
SPECIES: *Sequoia sempervirens*
HABITAT: Coastal temperate woodlands,
to 600 m above sea level
DISTRIBUTION: Pacific coast of North
America, from south-west Oregon to
central California
KEY FEATURE: Tallest living thing

VITAL STATISTICS

A WORLD IN BLOOM

FLOWERING PLANTS ARE BY FAR THE MOST SUCCESSFUL AND WIDESPREAD OF ALL PLANT GROUPS. They are represented in every type of habitat and have found a foothold in all corners of the Earth, from the tropics to the Arctic and even in small numbers in the Antarctic.

Contrary to the 'open-seeded' gymnosperms (see page 20), flowering plants, known as angiosperms, enclose their seeds in a fruit, an adaptation that ensures that the seed is protected during dispersal from the parent plant. The seed's fleshy coating also entices animals and insects to eat them. In this way, the seeds usually pass unharmed through the carrier and are deposited a distance away from the parent plant.

In terms of the evolution of plants, the angiosperms are relative

BEE MAGNETS
Sunflowers are mainly pollinated by honeybees, and farmers rely on the industrious insects for a good harvest of seeds.

newcomers. Given their delicate structures, fossils of early angiosperms are rare, with usually only the tougher parts, such as seeds and fruits, surviving in the rock strata. The first flowering plant on record is *Archaefructus sinensis*, which lived around 125 million years ago and was fossilised in stone in north-east China. Scientists believe the plant, which contained seeds in an immature fruit, probably lived in shallow freshwater with its flowers extending above the surface. It is thought that its closest modern relative is the water lily. Fossilised pollen grains date earlier primitive flowering plants to the end of the Jurassic period, around 140 million years ago. Today, there are about 250 000 known kinds of angiosperm – with hundreds more discovered every year – and they make up over 80 per cent of the entire plant kingdom.

Pollen carriers

Flowers are essentially sexual organs and it is their method of reproduction that has made the angiosperms such a success. The advent of flowers heralded a more reliable and targeted transfer of pollen than wind-borne pollination. By their colour, shape and scent, flowers are able to attract pollinators, such as insects, birds, bats and even lizards.

When a pollinator, such as a bee, visits a flower, it receives a dusting of pollen from the male anthers (see page 27). At the next flower on its route, this pollen is transferred to the stigma, the female part of the flower that receives the pollen. This method of pollination encourages cross-fertilisation, which helps to increase the genetic variety of a species. As a reward for its services, the pollinator receives a sugary solution called nectar, which is stored in nectaries usually deep within the plant.

Some pollinators, such as honeybees, also collect a share of the protein-rich pollen.

The various flowering plants compete fiercely to attract pollinators, adopting a range of strategies to get their attention. Petals in a palette of colours act as beacons to passing pollinators, while many blooms emit sweet perfumes, to which insects are particularly sensitive, detecting them at great distances. The bee orchids have perfected mimicry, looking and smelling exactly like female bees to attract male bees, which try to mate with the flowers.

Once they are lured in, it is the shape and structure of the flower that ensure that the pollinators receive their all-important cargo of

pollen. The flowers of freesia, honeysuckle and jasmine, for example, are trumpet-shaped, with the nectar stored at the bottom of the tube. Common toadflax, meanwhile, has a flower that is the perfect size to accommodate a bumblebee. When the insect lands on the flower, it pushes open the petals and shuffles forward, just reaching the long, pointed spur at the back of the flower where the toadflax holds its nectar. Thus, in return for a drink of nectar, flowering plants ensure that their pollen is not squandered on the breeze but reaches the female parts of another plant of the same species.

The flowers of some plants, such as grasses, still release their pollen onto the wind, producing large quantities of tiny grains to ensure success. Since they do not need to attract pollinators, their flowers tend to be small and inconspicuous.

VARIATIONS ON A THEME

WITH AN EXQUISITE BEAUTY THAT HAS PLEASED HUMAN EYES THROUGHOUT THE AGES, FLOWERS ARE NONETHELESS FINE-TUNED MECHANISMS FOR REPRODUCTION. They come in a cornucopia of colours, shapes and sizes, all directed at attracting the pollinators. There are giants such as the flowers of rafflesia, which measure up to 1 m across, down to the microscopic blooms of the duckweed *Wolffia globosa*, a plant so small it can pass through the eye of a needle. Flowers are shaped like bells, trumpets, funnels or bowls, some are star-shaped, some are long and thin, some others have protruding lips.

The petals – from the Greek *petalon*, meaning 'leaf' – are commonly the most showy and conspicuous part of a flower and exist in tremendous variation. The dog rose has a simple arrangement of five pink-coloured petals encircling the yellow male and female reproductive organs. After fertilisation, the ovary swells and reddens to form a rose-hip, full of maturing, furry seeds. In the foxglove, the petals have fused to form a bell-shaped flower, whereas the flowers of the sweet pea are irregularly shaped, the four lower petals joining together to make a protruding 'lip', or platform, while the larger fifth petal forms a curved 'hood' over the top of the flower. This shape ensures that the pollen stays well hidden within and is only collected by insects that land on the platform, opening up the flower as they

do so. The petals of some plants, including many orchids, have patterns, known as nectar guides, that act like signposts to direct the pollinators to their cache of nectar.

Looking as much a work of art as of nature, the passionflower has large exotic purple, red and white flowers whose components are said to symbolise the passion of Christ. With their flattened heads, the three red stigmas represent the nails in the cross, while the five stamens spread out in the shape of a star stand for Christ's wounds. The halo around Christ's head – or alternatively the crown of thorns – is seen in the corona, the double row of thin, purple filaments surrounding the flower. The passionflower's five white petals and five sepals stand for 10 of the apostles – there is no Peter and no Judas.

Another exotic beauty is the *Strelitzia*, or bird-of-paradise plant, of South Africa. Its flowers are made up of three upright orange sepals and three vivid blue petals, two of which join to form an arrowhead, while the third stores nectar at the base of the flower. The large, showy bloom attracts sunbirds, which land on the arrowhead seeking a drink of nectar. As they reach down into the flower they brush the stamen, picking up pollen on their feet and feathers.

A matter of presentation

There are also variations in the way flowers are attached to the plant. Tulips, for instance, are borne singly at the top of a stem, while others, including the mophead hydrangeas, put out tight, domed clusters of flowers, or inflorescences. The flowers of *Kniphofia* are tightly packed in flame-coloured 'spikes' giving them their common name of red-hot pokers, while the bell-shaped

BELL-SHAPED *The speckles on the inside lip of foxglove flowers direct pollinating insects towards the nectar at the end of the tube.*

UMBRELLA-LIKE *Grouping its flowers in flat-topped clusters, or umbels, cow parsley makes sure that its tiny blooms get noticed.*

COMPLEX *Orchid petals are intricately arranged. A series of lines and dots direct potential pollinators towards the nectar – and the flower's sexual organs.*

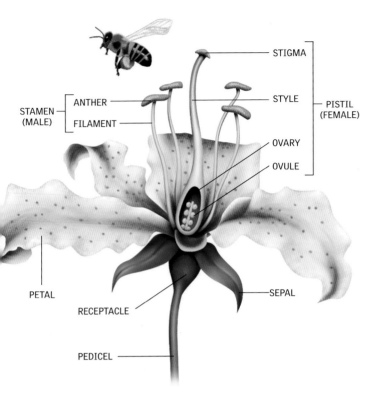

STIGMA

STYLE

ANTHER

STAMEN
(MALE)

FILAMENT

PISTIL
(FEMALE)

OVARY

OVULE

PETAL

RECEPTACLE

SEPAL

PEDICEL

PARTS OF A FLOWER A flower produces the plant's sex cells (gametes). The male part of the flower is called the stamen. Here male gametes are found in pollen produced in the anthers. Pollen grains land on the stigma, then pass down the style to the ovary to fertilise the female gametes, or ovules, which become seeds when fertilised. The female parts are collectively known as the pistil. The male and female parts are enclosed by petals, which are themselves enclosed by leaf-like sepals forming a protective layer when the flower is in bud. Some flowers produce both male and female sex cells (as here), while others have separate male and female flowers, either on the same plant, or on different plants.

flowers of bluebells are loosely grouped on delicate, pendulous stems. The tiny flowers of cow parsley are arranged in a large, flat-topped inflorescence – or umbel – that provides a conspicuous landing pad for pollinating insects.

Sometimes what looks like a single flower turns out to be hundreds of tiny flowers packed together. This is the case with many asters, including the sunflower, *Helianthus annuus*. With its distinctive dark centre surrounded by large petals it looks like a single flower, but it is in fact a large flowerhead composed of numerous individual flowers, or florets. The 'disc florets' clustered in the middle are surrounded by a ring of 'ray florets' with large, bright yellow petals. The flowerhead's structure becomes more obvious after fertilisation, when the central disc is a mass of seeds, each seed belonging to one disc floret.

Another group of plants with deceptive blooms is the arum family, the most familiar of which, the arum lily from South Africa, is made up of a pure-white trumpet wrapped around an upright yellow rod. The white trumpet looks like a giant petal but is in fact a modified leaf called a spathe. The yellow rod, called a spadix, comprises a central fleshy axis carrying hundreds of tiny flowers, usually arranged in bands of males and females, with the latter flowers closest to the base.

The arum lily exudes a charming fragrance, but many other members of this family are, to our noses at least, malodorous. Instead of attracting nectar-seeking insects, these plants aim to lure pollinators on the lookout for dead meat. The dead horse arum, for example, has a large purplish pink spathe that emits a stench like rotting flesh. Blowflies cannot resist and crawl deep inside, brushing past male and female flowers at the base of the spadix.

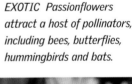

SPIKES The flowers on the densely packed spires of red-hot pokers open in sequence, from bottom to top, encouraging insects to return.

EXOTIC Passionflowers attract a host of pollinators, including bees, butterflies, hummingbirds and bats.

COMPOSITE Daisy flowers are made up of lots of tiny yellow central 'disc florets' surrounded by white 'ray florets'.

BLOOMING WILDERNESS Against a
backdrop of rugged peaks and ice-filled
lakes, wildflowers, including fireweeds
and lupins, grow in profusion in Alaska's
Russell Fiord Wilderness.

PLACE INVADERS

GOING WITH THE FLOW A vibrant claret cup cactus has found a foothold in the black, fissured lava of the Valley of Fires State Park, New Mexico.

ALTHOUGH ROOTED TO THE SPOT, plants are remarkably adept at spreading out, using their seeds, spores or creeping stems to colonise new terrain. The first plants to arrive are the pioneers – opportunists such as mosses and lichens, or annuals whose many seeds are carried far and wide by parachutes of fine hairs. Other species then turn up, eventually outcompeting the pioneers, either by growing taller and shading them out, or by being better suited to the changing soil or climate. Over time, several communities will come and go in this manner, a process called succession, until eventually relative stability is reached in a 'climax community'.

Taming the dunes

A good place to observe this process of plant colonisation, establishment and extinction in action is in coastal areas where there is a well-developed dune system. The pioneers colonise the inhospitable strandline just above the high-water mark. Poor in nutrients and organic matter, the sand here also carries salt from sea spray. Freshwater is in short supply and many dune plants are adapted accordingly. Sea rocket has fleshy leaves to store water, while the leaves of sand couch-grass and lyme-grass have a waxy coating to reduce water loss. The plants also make use of dew formed on the sand at night, and many species have long, vertical roots that reach down to the water table.

Clinging on with their roots for dear life, the pioneers begin to hold some of the sand in place, forming a windbreak so that more sand is deposited. As the dune grows in height, marram grass, a crucial dune-fixing plant, arrives on the scene. Like all grasses, it grows from the base, not the tips, so its shoots can push up through the sand even when they have been buried. The grass spreads outwards at a rate of 3 m per year and grows so rapidly upwards that it can tolerate a rise in the sand level of 1 m per year.

Inland from the strand line is the zone called the yellow dunes. Here the vegetation is still patchy and most of the surface is loose, open sand, but coastal specialists such as sand sedge, sea holly, sea bindweed and sea spurge take root here. The soil conditions begin to improve in this zone. The dead remains of pioneer plants help to hold water and trap nutrients, enabling less specialised plants, such as dandelions, ragworts and thistles, to colonise the area. Behind the crests of the yellow dunes lie the grey dunes, a more sheltered habitat where sand is no longer deposited and marram grass gives way to sand-dune screw moss and greyish-coloured lichens, such as cladonias and dog lichen. With the sand now fixed and organic matter building up, summer-flowering plants, including bird's-foot trefoil,

cowslip, viper's bugloss, pyramidal orchid and common centaury, take root. Still further inland, the organic matter in the soil has built up enough to support pasture and grasses, as well as shrubs such as hawthorn, elder, sea buckthorn, bramble and gorse. In between the dunes, hollows, known as slacks, may be marshy and even contain pools of freshwater, providing a natural habitat for marsh flowers such as marsh helleborine, mounds of creeping willow and even rushes and sedges. Woodland forms the final stage of the coastal dune succession.

Back to nature

Plant colonisation also takes place in the man-made world. Abandoned buildings can be reclaimed by nature in a relatively short space of time. Windblown seeds lodge in crannies, where organic matter builds up, eventually holding enough sustenance for seeds to germinate. Soon roots are penetrating down through cracks in the concrete to reach the soil. Meanwhile, the elements take their toll on the building, and roofs collapse, creating more light and space for new plants to exploit.

MOVING IN Plants invade and colonise man-made structures, such as this abandoned truck in Hawaii.

PLANT LOOKALIKES

WITH THEIR LEAF-LIKE FRONDS AND WHAT APPEAR TO BE ROOTS, seaweeds were once thought to be members of the plant kingdom. They are not, even though they have the green pigment chlorophyll which, like plants, they used in photosynthesis (see page 36). Seaweeds are in fact algae, their root-like structures – known as holdfasts – act simply as anchors, while their fronds do not have the vascular system of true leaves, since all parts can absorb the fluids, nutrients and gases they require directly from the water.

Long stalk-like structures called stipes carry numerous fronds that reach up to the surface of the water towards the light. Other seaweeds form flat sheets or whip-like blades; still others are made up of chains of bead-like cells, which in the tropical *Ventricaria ventricosa* are up to 3 cm across and resemble marbles lying on the rocks. Seaweeds are often known as macroalgae, an appropriate epithet given the enormous size that some attain. The giant kelp *Macrocystis pyrifera* begins life as a microscopic spore but can grow as much as a metre a day to reach a length of around 60 m, forming dense underwater forests, which harbour an abundance of marine life.

At the other end of the size scale are the microalgae, or phytoplankton. Although microscopic, these single-celled algae are vital for life on Earth, producing an estimated 50–75 per cent of the world's oxygen through photosynthesis, while absorbing much of the carbon dioxide in the Earth's atmosphere. Some live in ponds and lakes, others as green slime on rocks and trees, but most drift in great clouds on the ocean currents. Among the latter are the dinoflagellates, which have whip-like tails that propel them through the water like spinning tops.

Fooled by fungi

Early naturalists also lumped fungi with plants, but the characteristics of fungi are different enough that they are now placed in their own kingdom in the classification of living things. For although fungi pop up out of the ground like emerging plant stems, they have nothing that resembles leaves or flowers, their cell walls are made of chitin (a horny substance found in the exoskeletons of such things as insects and crustaceans) instead

SHOWER PROOF: Rain bounces off the delicate parasol-like caps of a pair of Paddestoelen *mushrooms. The cap helps to protect the gills and spores underneath.*

of cellulose, they feed on animal and plant tissue rather than through photosynthesis – and they can grow in the dark.

Fungi also have life cycles quite unlike anything else on Earth. For the most part, they remain hidden, forming an underground mass of tangled threads (hyphae) collectively called a mycelium. The mushrooms and toadstools that emerge above ground are the fruiting bodies of the fungi. They are the equivalent of flowers, but instead of shedding pollen, they send spores adrift on the breeze. The fungi may distribute these spores by shaking them out of their gills or, like the puffballs, produce mini explosions to release the spores in a vertical 'puff'.

Fungi species number in the thousands and include the antibiotics, yeasts and moulds, as well as the rusts, which cause serious damage to crops and other plants. Another group are the mycorrhizal fungi that live in the soil among the roots of plants. They form a symbiotic partnership with plants, giving them nutrients in return for sugars made by the plants. Above all, fungi are Earth's great decomposers and recyclers, feeding on dead organic matter and making it available in the food chain.

The odd couple

If algae and fungi are perplexing to classify, the lichens are even stranger, because they are not a single organism but a working partnership between a fungus and an alga. The basis of the relationship is that fungi can break down soil and rocks to gain nutrients, but they cannot photosynthesise and make sugars. Algae can do the opposite. Over time, the fungi enclosed the algae and to all intents and purposes the partners began to function as a single entity. The fungal skin protects the algae within from drying out and the fungus secretes substances that shield the alga from harmful ultraviolet light.

SLOW-GROWERS Patches of lichen cling to a dry-stone wall in the English Lake District. Lichens spread radially at a rate of just 1–6 mm a year.

ON THE ROCKS A sinuous mass of seaweed covers these rocks in the Orkney Islands in Scotland.

The relationship has stood the test of time, going back millions of years to the first forms of life on land. And it is a winning partnership, with around 30 000 known species of lichen, seen in numerous forms, from orange, yellow or purple blister-like encrustations on rocks, tree trunks or soil, to green, 'leafy', branching clumps – known as the beard lichens – that look more like moss or low-growing plants. And they are able to live where nothing else can. In the Arctic, the lichen known as reindeer moss provides reindeer with much of their sustenance in winter. In the heat of the Atacama Desert, lichens attach themselves to the surface of cacti. They survive by drying out and suspending all activity, then quickly rehydrating at the first sign of moisture. Two species of lichen (*Rhizocarpon geographicum* and *Xanthoria elegans*) have even survived an unprotected brush with outer space. In November 2005, the European Space Agency exposed the lichens to open space for 15 days. Despite the potentially damaging conditions of a total vacuum, wide fluctuations of temperature and the full spectrum of cosmic radiation, including UV light, the lichens showed no sign of damage.

STRATEGIES
FOR LIFE

2

ONE OF THE MOST ASTONISHING POWERS OF PLANTS IS THEIR ABILITY TO CAPTURE SUNLIGHT AND CARBON DIOXIDE IN THEIR LEAVES, and then use them to make sugars and starches. Unlike animals, plants cannot move around to find food, so they must make the best of where they are. Since sunlight and water are key to their survival, they have developed various strategies for getting their share. In the rain forest, where competition for light is fierce, climbers, such as rattans, use other plants for support as they reach for the Sun. In the desert, fleshy stems and waxy leaves or spines are the order of the day as plants seek to conserve water, like these jumping cholla and saguaro cacti in the Sonoran Desert of the south-western USA. A few plants steal the nutrients they need from other plants or capture insects in traps to supplement their diets.

SOLAR POWER

THERE IS ONE FUNDAMENTAL DIFFERENCE BETWEEN PLANTS AND ANIMALS: most plants manufacture their own food, while animals rely on eating plants or other animals, or both. The secret of the plants' self-sufficiency is the process of photosynthesis. Arguably the single most important chemical reaction on Earth, photosynthesis is what enables plants to make the food they need by tapping into the energy of sunlight. Not only is photosynthesis the basis of the food chain and the chief way in which energy is captured from the Sun, it also generates oxygen – the vital component of the air we breathe – as a by-product.

LIFE FORCE Sunlight on green leaves triggers photosynthesis, the reaction that powers life on Earth.

In essence, photosynthesis uses energy from the Sun to turn carbon dioxide (from the air) and water (taken up from a plant's roots) into sugar and oxygen. To think of it as a recipe, it could be stated like this: take six molecules of water, six molecules of carbon dioxide, add some sunlight and the result is six molecules of glucose (a type of sugar) and six molecules of oxygen.

The process is complicated, but can be generalised into two phases. The first is a light-dependent stage, which takes place only during daylight hours. Chlorophyll, a green pigment in leaves, captures energy from sunlight and stores it in 'carrier' molecules. At the same time, water drawn up from the plant's roots is split

CAPTURING SUNLIGHT Photosynthesis takes place in tiny grains, called chloroplasts, which are distributed through the layers of cells sandwiched between a leaf's upper and lower surfaces. The chloroplasts all contain chlorophyll, the green pigment that absorbs sunlight and converts it into chemical energy, and enzymes, which use this energy to make sugars. There may be as many as 100 chloroplasts in each cell. Water for the process is transported from the roots, arriving in the leaf through xylem vessels (see page 39) in the veins. Carbon dioxide enters through pores, called stomata (singular: stomatum), in the leaf's skin, and the by-product of the process, oxygen, exits into the atmosphere by the same route, through the stomata.

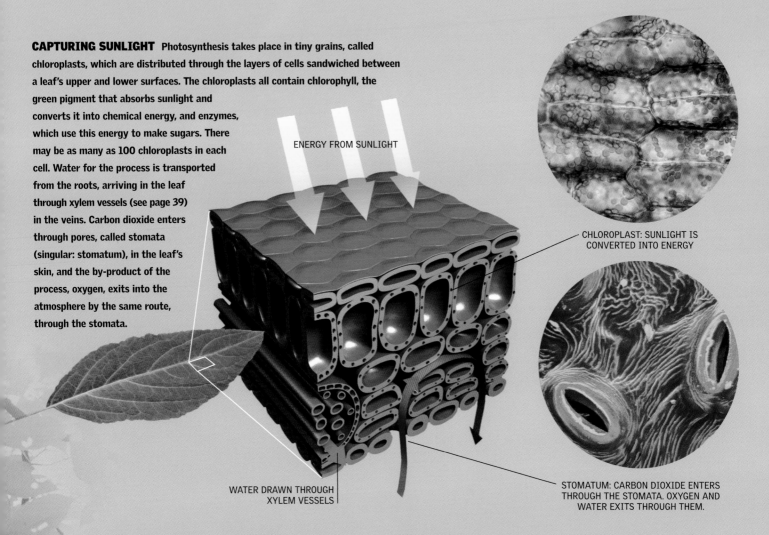

ENERGY FROM SUNLIGHT

CHLOROPLAST: SUNLIGHT IS CONVERTED INTO ENERGY

WATER DRAWN THROUGH XYLEM VESSELS

STOMATUM: CARBON DIOXIDE ENTERS THROUGH THE STOMATA. OXYGEN AND WATER EXITS THROUGH THEM.

into oxygen, which is released into the atmosphere, and hydrogen. During the second phase – which does not require light, so can happen during the day or night – the energy-carrying molecules and hydrogen are used to convert carbon dioxide into glucose.

When thousands of glucose molecules are joined up into long chains, they form molecules of either starch or cellulose. The starches are energy stores, usually deposited in the roots until the plant needs to draw on them, at which point it breaks them down into glucose units. Cellulose is used as a structural element in the plant's cell walls. By adding other minerals taken up from the soil, such as nitrogen and sulphur, the plant is able to manufacture other kinds of molecules, which make up the proteins and tissues it needs to grow.

Many shades of colour

Chlorophyll is the main pigment by which plants capture energy from sunlight, but they have other 'accessory' pigments, called carotenoids, in shades of orange and yellow. The carotenoids absorb slightly different wavelengths of light and so broaden the spectrum of light energy that can be fixed through photosynthesis. Plants also sometimes contain purple-red pigments, called anthocyanins, although these do not take part in photosynthesis.

A few plants use pigments to reflect light back into the leaves. Some types of begonia, for example, have a layer of purple cells on the undersides of their leaves. In the wild, begonias live on the shady floor of tropical forests, where light is scarce, and the purple layer reflects light back through a leaf to the upper surface. This ensures another pass of light through the photosynthesising pigments in the leaf's upper layers.

In the autumn, leaves begin to change into a range of colours from golden yellows to browns and vivid shades of red. This is the result of a process called senescence, in which chlorophyll breaks down within the leaf, revealing the other pigments. But there is more to it than that. Plants start breaking down their chlorophyll before leaf fall to reabsorb the nitrogen it contains and store the nitrogen for the next growing season. At the same time, research shows that they are actively making purple-red anthocyanins in the leaves. In combination with the yellow carotenoids already within the leaves and the gradual breakdown of chlorophyll, the production of purple-red anthocyanins leads to the striking and varied shades of autumnal colour.

Why are the plants making anthocyanins in leaves that are about to drop? It seems like a waste of effort. Researchers at Harvard University in the USA are hoping to discover the reason, and have come up with several theories. One suggests that as the plant breaks down its chlorophyll and reabsorbs its nitrogen, it produces anthocyanins, which are strong antioxidants, as a sunscreen to protect the leaves from ultraviolet radiation.

GREEN ENGINEERING

PLUMBING SYSTEM Water and nutrients travel through leaves along a branching network of veins, as seen in this begonia leaf.

LEAVES ARE NATURE'S SOLAR PANELS. Instead of bearing rows of photovoltaic cells that convert sunlight into electricity, they are packed with chloroplasts that turn sunlight into sugar and the other substances that a plant needs for growth. In addition, leaves are the 'lungs' of a plant, allowing carbon dioxide to flow in and oxygen to flow out. Extraordinary pieces of engineering, leaves are perfectly designed to carry out both these functions.

A close examination of a leaf shows that it is covered in veins. In some plants, such as irises, the veins run parallel to one

SIMPLE OVAL Hostas are grown for their large luscious leaves with prominent veins.

STRAP-SHAPED Daffodil leaves appear with the flowers and elongate as the flowers fade.

SWORD-SHAPED Iris leaves are long and pointed at the tip. They grow in a fan around the flowering stem.

LEAFLETS Fern leaves, as in this lady fern, are made up of numerous tiny leaflets.

WATER BUTT Many bromeliads form a rosette with their leaves to catch water.

FURRY The tiny hairs covering mullein leaves help to reduce water loss in hot Mediterranean summers.

FLESHY STORE Madagascar's Alluaudia procera *endures drought by storing water in its leaves. Sharp thorns keep would-be browsers at bay.*

another along the length of the leaf; in others, the leaves have branching networks. Besides giving the leaf the structure that holds it in shape, the veins are also its plumbing system. Inside the veins, specialised cells, called xylem cells, link up to form xylem vessels – long, hollow tubes that carry water and minerals up from the roots. Strengthened by a woody substance called lignin, the xylem vessels are often the last parts of a leaf to decay; they form the familiar 'skeleton' seen in a leaf that has almost rotted away. Alongside the xylem tubes, a second network, consisting of phloem vessels, carries the products of photosynthesis – sugars and starches – away from the leaves to the parts of the plant where they are needed.

Plant pores

Leaves 'breathe' via openings called stomata, which are usually located on their undersides. When open, the stomata let carbon dioxide in and oxygen and water out. The evaporation of water through the stomata is called transpiration and is essential for the circulation of water through the plant. As water molecules evaporate from the leaves, more water is sucked up the xylem tubes from the roots (see page 22). This means that the flow of water in a plant is always one-way – upwards.

In dry conditions, a plant may not be able to replenish the water being lost through its leaves, in which case it has to regulate the rate of evaporation. Each of the stomata is protected by two guard cells, one on either side. These are plumped up when water is plentiful, keeping the stomata open. If too much water is being lost, the guard cells lose pressure and become flaccid, closing the stomata and preventing further water loss.

All shapes and sizes

Although they all serve the same function, leaves have developed in a huge variety of forms. Some, such as beech leaves, consist of a single blade, while those of the ash have numerous leaflets. Leaves may be rounded, oval or strap-shaped. Some have lobes, such as maple leaves; others, like horse chestnut leaves, are palmate – looking rather like a human hand, with leaflets or lobes radiating from a single point. The edges of leaves may be smooth or they may be serrated like a knife, and they can be arranged in numerous ways on the stem.

Botanists cannot explain why all of the variations have developed – why, for example, two trees growing side by side in the same conditions, such as an oak and a sycamore, have leaves that are so dissimilar in shape. Yet some of the differences clearly help plants to survive in particular habitats. Conifers, for instance, are adapted to life in cold, dry environments, where their small, needle-like leaves with a waxy coating help to reduce water loss. Deciduous plants, living in more moderate and moist conditions, can afford large, flat leaves with a more porous skin.

LIGHT HITS
SURFACE OF LEAF

GREEN IS
REFLECTED FROM
THE LEAF SURFACE

ALL OTHER COLOURS
OF THE SPECTRUM
ARE ABSORBED

Deep in the shady parts of tropical forests, a family of ferns, called the filmy ferns, has some of the most delicate leaves in the world. In plants with bulkier leaves, sunlight is diffused as it passes through the different layers of cells in each leaf. By contrast, the feathery fingers of a filmy fern's leaves are just one cell thick, which means that they gather the available light more efficiently than bulkier leaves would. Since the tropical air is humid, the ferns do not need a thick cuticle against water loss.

At the other end of the scale are pebble plants, which live in the Namib Desert of south-western Africa. For them, water conservation is a major challenge. Rainfall in the Namib may be less than 10 cm a year, so the plants have honed down their foliage to just two stumpy leaves, with the remainder of the plant buried under the soil. Containing fleshy tissue for water storage, the leaves are also flat and rounded to minimise transpiration and, like many desert plants, they open their stomata at night when conditions are cooler, reducing water loss by 90 per cent.

Size matters

The adage 'the bigger the better' is definitely true for some plants, which have developed enormous leaves, presenting huge surface areas for photosynthesis. This adaptation is often seen in floor-dwelling plants growing in mature tropical rain forests, where light levels may be low. These include *Gunnera manicata*, whose home in the wild is the rain forests of Brazil. Sometimes called prickly rhubarb and grown in British gardens principally for its foliage, it has serrated leaves that are 2 m wide growing

on equally long, thick, thorny stalks – the umbrella-like structures can provide handy shelter in a tropical downpour. Another tropical species with even larger leaves – the largest undivided leaves in the plant kingdom – is *Alocasia macrorrhizos*, or giant taro. This is a Malaysian relative of the arum lily (see page 27), widely grown for its edible rhizomes and shoots. At over 3 m long, each heart-shaped taro leaf has a surface area of 6 m^2.

In Australia, the problem is an excess, not a lack, of burning sunshine. The island continent's native acacias and eucalyptus trees have responded to this by holding their leaves edgeways to the Sun to avoid receiving too much light. For a similar reason, *Alluaudia* trees in Madagascar's spiny forests – desert-dry zones of dense, thorny thickets – have developed lots of small, fleshy leaves that cling to the trees' spiky trunks. Appearing in the wet season, these leaves drop during dry periods, which can last for a year or more. Like the horsetails (see page 19) and most cacti, *Alluaudia* trees undertake photosynthesis through their stems and branches.

Leaves have also evolved in shapes that deter predators. Some use physical countermeasures, such as spines and hairs. Others use trickery. In Central and South America, female *Heliconius* butterflies lay their eggs on the leaves of the passion vine, the food plant for their caterpillars. This is bad for the plant, since the larvae may strip it of its foliage, so it tricks the butterflies by growing yellow egg-like knobs at the base of some of its leaves. A visiting butterfly sees these decoys and thinks that another female has beaten her to this particular plant. Laying her own eggs there would lead to competition for food among the caterpillars, so she lays her eggs elsewhere. Passion vine leaves and tissues are also laced with toxins; the butterflies are immune to them, but they act as a defence against other herbivores. Many other plants carry poisons in their tissues which can be lethal (see page 115).

Tree pond life

Even though water is an essential requirement for plants, it is usually absorbed through the roots, not the leaves. Normally, the structure and arrangement of the leaves' veins and tissues cause water to pour along them and then drip off their tips, rinsing off any dust that might clog the leaf surface and interfere with the take-up of carbon dioxide.

This system is of no use to epiphytic bromeliads (see page 44), which grow on the branches of tall rain-forest trees, with their roots wrapped around the branches. As they have no contact with the ground, the bromeliads are obliged to capture water via their leaves. Growing in tight rosettes around a central bud, the leaves form mini-ponds in which rainwater accumulates, providing not only moisture but also nutrients. Birds and small animals come to drink from the pools and sometimes leave their droppings in the water, while other creatures may lay their eggs in it. The debris falls to the bottom of the pool, providing the plants with minerals that would otherwise be out of reach. In these plants, the roots function principally as anchors and not as entry points for nutrients. Instead, water and minerals are taken into the plants by way of hairs or scales attached to the leaves in the rosette.

SOME OF THE LARGEST LEAVES IN THE PLANT KINGDOM ARE THOSE OF AFRICA'S RAFFIA PALMS – UP TO 25 M LONG AND 3 M WIDE IN THE CASE OF ONE SPECIES, *RAPHIA REGALIS*.

Africans use the fibres of these huge leaves to make raffia skirts and capes, nowadays mainly reserved for ceremonial costumes. They also weave the fibres into hats, baskets and mats, and tap the plants' sugary sap to make palm wine and a distilled spirit.

Unlike conifers and deciduous trees, the 28 raffia species do not lay down secondary thickening (wood) in their trunks. A young palm grows radially (outwards) for a few years, then it begins to push upwards. From then on, it more or less maintains its width, reaching heights of up to 18 m. When it is about to bloom – which happens after 20–40 years – most of the palm's resources go into making a large inflorescence (flower head), emerging from the top of the trunk. Composed of thousands of tiny flowers, the inflorescence may be a tall towering structure or long and pendulous. Male and female flowers are held on the same flower head, the large showy males at the tips and the small females at the base. Eventually, when the plant is fertilised and fruit set, the palm dies.

VITAL STATISTICS

CLASS: Liliopsida
ORDER: Arecales
SPECIES: *Raphia*
HABITAT: Wet, tropical regions
DISTRIBUTION: Central Africa and Madagascar; one South American species
KEY FEATURE: Very large leavess

RAFFIA PALM

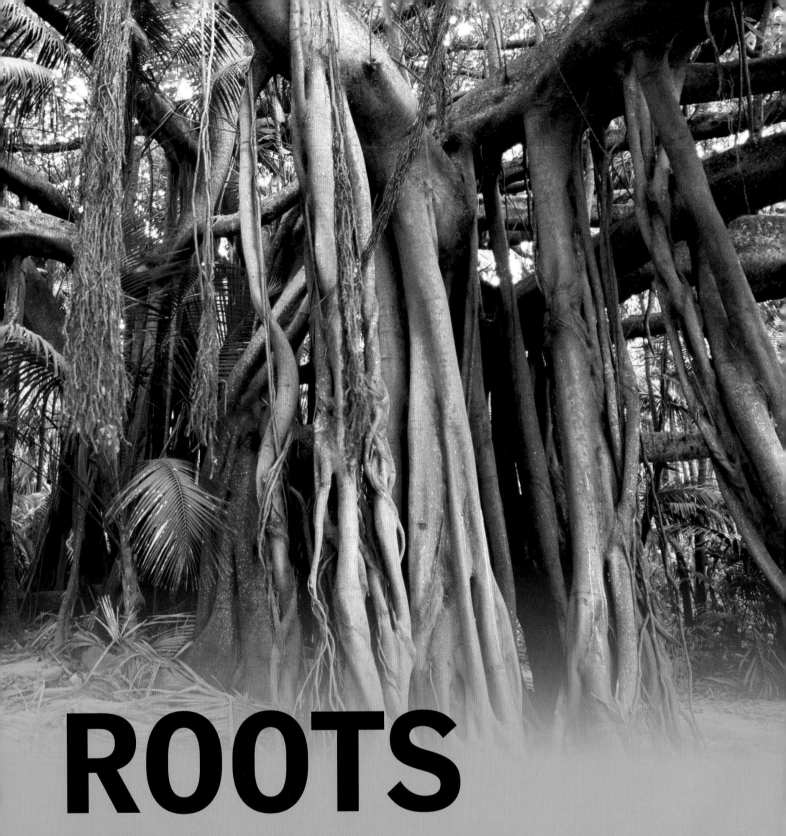

ROOTS

PLANTS ARE AS BUSY UNDERGROUND AS THEY ARE ABOVE. While their shoots and stems grow upwards towards the light, down below they are building networks of roots. There are two types of root system. One consists of a thick, sparsely branched taproot, such as that which makes up the edible parts of carrots and parsnips. The other is a more fibrous, many-branched lateral system, which weaves its way through a large volume of soil, as found in grasses. Both types act as anchors – taproots are especially good at preventing a plant from blowing over, while fibrous, branching roots resist being pulled up. Many plants have a combination of the two, first growing a taproot, from which numerous fibrous roots then spread out. As these roots develop, they form a tangled, interwoven network that helps to hold the soil together and is important in preventing soil erosion.

ROOTING STRANGLER The huge aerial roots of the banyan tree form trunk-like pillars that enable the tree to spread through the forest. The banyan is a fig, which germinates as an epiphyte in the branches of a host tree. As it grows, it sends down aerial roots to the ground, eventually creating a massive structure that can do without the host tree – usually strangled in the process.

PLANT ON A WIRE Air plants grow in unlikely places, including telephone lines. They take in water from the atmosphere and nutrients from the dust that lands on them.

The shape and extent of a plant's root structure varies with the type of soil and its moisture content. Where water is reasonably plentiful, lateral, spreading systems are often just a few centimetres below the surface of the ground. Desert plants often have very long taproots that descend to the water table far below the surface of the ground – the tamarisk tree of Asia and the Mediterranean region can reach down to 50 m. Surprisingly, many trees, even some large ones, do not have taproots; they support themselves with an extensive mat of fibrous roots, which forms a broad, if shallow, footing. In temperate zones, these systems tend to fan out around the base of the trunk in a circle that widens as the tree's leafy canopy enlarges. The water-absorbing tips of the roots stay directly beneath the area known as the 'drip zone', where rain falls off the leaves of the canopy above.

Some trees are 'thirstier' than others, a key consideration when building on clay-rich soil, whose volume depends on its water content. If trees are extracting large amounts of water in spring and summer, this will cause the soil to shrink, leading to subsidence in nearby buildings. On the other hand, felling the trees might leave too much water, resulting in 'heave' as the sodden clay swells up. Thirsty trees include eucalyptus and white willow, while hazel and magnolia have some of the lowest water demands.

Many-layered structure

In cross-section, a root consists of several layers, which can be seen clearly in a disc of sliced carrot. The inner, darker region of the slice contains the plumbing system; like stems and leaves, roots contain both xylem vessels, along which water moves up the plant, and phloem vessels, which bring nutrients and sugars back to the roots. Surrounding this central section is a layer of cortex, where food is stored. The cortex is enclosed in turn by the epidermis, the skin that we peel away when preparing a carrot for the pot.

Growth and elongation of a root takes place at its very tip, in an area of rapidly dividing cells called the 'apical meristem'. A layer of cells, called the root cap, protects the tip against the abrasiveness of the soil. These cells are sloughed off, then replaced by new cells produced by the apical meristem. Slightly further up the root is the region where water is absorbed. Here, numerous delicate hairs grow out from the epidermis, greatly increasing the root's surface area and enabling it to absorb more

PROPPED UP A maize plant's prop roots grow out from the main stem to prevent the plant from toppling over.

water. The root hairs find water in tiny pockets between particles of soil, soaking it up along with the dissolved nutrients it contains. The water then passes through the epidermal cells and into the cortex, finally reaching the central xylem, through which it is carried up into the plant.

Gripping and propping

Some plants have adapted their roots to do other jobs besides those of absorbing water and nutrients. Epiphytes, such as the air plants of the *Tillandsia* genus, have roots that are adapted to a soil-less lifestyle, since they spend their entire lives perched on the branches of trees – or occasionally telephone wires. Their narrow leaves are covered with moisture-absorbing scales, giving them a silvery appearance. In other plants, shallow underground roots are unable to support the plant's weight and so need reinforcing.

Many species of tropical fig tree grow large, fin-like projections, called 'buttress' roots, at the base of their trunks; their task is to anchor the figs securely in the nutrient-poor tropical soil. The maize plant grows 'prop' roots to prevent it from falling over; these arch out from nodes on the plant's stem and enter the soil some distance from the main plant. Mangrove trees growing in tropical swamps use a similar strategy, as well as developing another set of specialised roots. In the thick, waterlogged mud of the mangrove swamps, the little pockets of air that are present in most soils do not exist, so the roots have no access to the oxygen they need. As a result, mangrove trees have developed aerial roots, or pneumatophores, that remain above the level of the mud. Oxygen passes through pores in these aerial roots and is carried right down to the growing tips of the submerged roots.

GETTING ENOUGH LIGHT

ANYONE LOOKING UP THROUGH THE CANOPY OF A MATURE TREE ON A SUMMER'S DAY WILL SEE HOW THE LEAVES FORM A GREEN CEILING. They fit together rather like a mosaic, every leaf maximising its exposure to sunlight without impinging on its neighbour. Just as the leaves fit together in the crown of a single tree, so the crowns of plants interlock in a wood or forest as they jostle for a position in the Sun, forming an almost seamless canopy. When a tree dies, it leaves a space in the canopy and the race is on for new young plants to fill the gap.

Since sunlight is essential for photosynthesis, plants strive to reach a spot where they can bask in it. Besides simply growing up and spreading out, they employ other strategies as well to grab their share of sunshine. Epiphytes perch among the pockets of decaying leaves and other organic matter found on the branches of trees, then hitch a ride skywards as the trees grow. Most epiphytes are not parasitic – all they need from their 'host' is a place to perch. Because they live adrift from the soil, they have developed their own ways of acquiring water and nutrients. Many epiphytes absorb water directly from the air or as it trickles down tree branches and trunks, taking up nutrients from this water and whatever else tumbles from above.

Epiphytic bromeliads gather water within their rosettes of leaves (see page 40), while epiphytic ferns, such as the bird's-nest fern (*Asplenium nidus*) and staghorn ferns of South-east Asia, trap falling plant matter among their fronds. The ferns send out roots from their stems that grow into this decaying debris to absorb the nutrients. Epiphytic orchids collect plant debris in a basket of intertwined aerial roots. Assisting the plants in finding and using any available minerals are special fungi, called mycorrhizal fungi, which live among their roots.

Although most epiphytic species live in hot, humid tropical rain forests, epiphytes occur all over the world and in many different groups of plants.

WOODLAND CARPET In the spring, before the temperate deciduous trees have grown leaves, Japanese dog's-tooth violets (right) make the most of the abundant light.

RAIN-FOREST COMPETITION Climbers and epiphytes scramble up trees to get a share of the Caribbean sunshine.

More than half of the 25 000 species of orchids are epiphytic, and there are even epiphytic cacti, including the various species of Christmas cacti, native to mountainous regions of Brazil.

The only way is up

Plants can also gain access to sunlight by climbing up to it, supporting themselves in various ways on the stems and trunks of other mature plants. Honeysuckle winds its whole stem around the supporting plant. The vines of the passionflower climb by sending out long, thin modified leaves, or tendrils, with touch-sensitive tips. When the tendril finds a suitable support, it begins to coil around it. As the vine grows, the next leaf up its stem puts out a tendril, which in its turn winds around the support. By this means, the plant makes it way upwards.

Plants in the grapevine family, such as Virginia creeper, have small suckers at the tips of their tendrils. By gripping the trunks of trees and even walls, these discs allow the vines to climb vertically. Once firmly attached to the support, the tendrils coil up tightly, pulling the whole vine in close. Hook climbers include the rambling roses – which snag their thorns into the leaves and stems of other plants – and the rattans of South-east Asia. Rattans send out barbed stems up to 175 m long that hook onto nearby trees. As well as helping them to scramble through and over tropical rain-forest vegetation, the barbs also protect the rattan stems from being eaten.

The Swiss cheese plant, native to the rain forests of Central America, is another prolific climber. Having germinated into a seedling on the forest floor, it wanders off into the shadow of the tallest tree it can find – instead of seeking light, as most shoots do. The cheese plant climbs the tree using specialised

HANGING GARDEN A dense community of epiphytic plants has established itself on a branch in the Costa Rican rain forest. Unlike parasitic plants, epiphytes do not normally draw nourishment from the host plant.

roots, called 'adventitious' roots. These emerge from the leaf nodes on the plant's stems and wrap around the host trunk, securing the plant as it journeys upwards. European ivy climbs in a similar way, sending out tufts of roots from the undersides of its stems. These strong attachments, anchored to any nook or cranny, enable ivy to clamber up vertical walls.

Light-seeking communities

The results of the diverse light-gathering strategies are best appreciated in tropical rain forests, where communities of plants form 'gardens in the sky'. The branches of large trees may support hundreds of spiky-leaved bromeliads, delicate ferns and wiry climbers, while Spanish moss (*Tillandsia usneoides*) hangs down in scruffy drifts. Although generally not parasitic and not directly damaging to the trees, epiphytes and climbers in large numbers do weigh their 'hosts' down. As a way of dealing with too many residents, some tropical rain-forest trees self-prune by simply dropping an overburdened branch to the floor. This is a catastrophe for the plants residing there, but nothing is wasted – as the plants die and break down, the forest recycles the nutrients contained in them. A branch of the same or a neighbouring tree will grow into the gap, and in time it will be covered by a new community of squatters.

DEADLY EMBRACES

PLANTS ARE NOT OFTEN THOUGHT OF AS HUNTERS ACTIVELY PURSUING PREY, yet in the case of the dodder vine, a hunter is exactly what it is. Native to Europe and temperate parts of Asia and North Africa, the dodder (*Cuscuta epithymum*) is a total parasite, taking all its sustenance from its chosen host. It has long, thin pinkish-white stems and tendrils – looking rather like spaghetti – which it sends out in all directions, moving past weak-stemmed plants and seeking only the healthiest specimens. When it has located a suitable host, the dodder penetrates the plant's stem with sucker-like structures called haustoria. It can then begin to siphon off water and nutrients. Because the dodder steals everything it needs from its host, it does not have to photosynthesise and so does without leaves. It begins life with roots, but these soon become unnecessary, wither and die.

Once the parasite has consumed as much as it can from a host plant, it moves on, probing for more fresh juicy stems to suck. Progressing from plant to plant, it need never touch the ground again, even though its stems may eventually reach a total length of almost 1 km. Sometimes, small white flowers dot the stems, resembling those of its distant relative, the morning glory.

Once a dodder vine has consumed as much as it can from a host plant, the parasite moves on, probing for fresh juicy stems to suck.

UNFRIENDLY HUG A dodder wraps its tendrils around a nettle plant, stealing sustenance as it goes.

Malodorous blossom

In the jungles of Sumatra and Borneo, *Rafflesia arnoldii* has gone one step further even than the dodder. As well as doing away with leaves and roots, *Rafflesia* has relinquished the need for stems, spending most of its life hidden inside those of its host. Its habitual 'victim' is an unremarkable-looking vine called *Tetrastigma*, whose tissues it penetrates, sending out a tangled network of filaments that spread through the plant, raiding its nutrients. There is no outward sign of the infestation, until the *Rafflesia* prepares to flower, and then it is hard to ignore. At a place where the host vine trails down to the jungle floor, a swelling appears on its stem. This growth is the parasite's flower bud and resembles a small, orange cabbage. Eventually, the five fleshy sepals unfurl to present a bloom 1 m across and up to 7 kg in weight. It is the largest flower in the plant kingdom and one of the foulest-smelling, emitting an odour of rotting meat to attract the flies that pollinate it.

Dodder and *Rafflesia* are total parasites, relying on the host plant for all of their nutrients and water. Mistletoes are only partly parasitic. Although they take some of their nutrients and all of their water from their host plant through haustoria on their roots, they have green leaves and can photosynthesise. There are more than a thousand species of mistletoe, most of which live in the tropics. Some grow on a variety of tree hosts, while others are limited to just

TREE SUCKERS Mistletoes are semi-parasitic. They take water from the tree they grow on, but make their own sugars through photosynthesis.

one species. Many are spread by birds, which eat mistletoe berries, then wipe their beaks or tails on the trees, depositing the seeds.

While the roots of most mistletoe species burrow into a host tree above ground, one species becomes a tree in its own right, carrying out its parasitism underground. In the dry summers of Western Australia, the most precious resource is water. The majority of plants die back during this season, to endure the long wait for rain, but not the 15 m tall Christmas tree, which owes its name to the glorious display of golden flowers it produces around Christmas time. The Christmas tree looks like any other tree, but while others are suffering the leaf-

curling effects of prolonged drought, it appears to be thriving. The reason for this lies in a system of far-reaching roots that steal water directly from the roots of other plants. Probing the soil beneath the parched earth, they detect another root and fix onto it, completely encircling it before they sever its water-carrying vessels and divert the precious liquid back to the Christmas tree. The roots cover great distances, up to 100 m away from the tree. Any type of plant can fall victim to the Christmas tree – its roots have even been known to penetrate underground electrical cables to the annoyance of Australian technicians.

A taste for flesh

Carnivorous plants sound like something from a science fiction movie, but there are several species of plant that capture and ingest animals – chiefly insects. Most of these plants are able to make

food from sunlight, but they grow in regions where the soil is poor in nutrients, so their diet of insects acts like a vitamin shot. They catch their prey by means of ingenious traps – once set, these enable the plants to wait for their next meal to arrive.

The pitcher plants, found mainly in South-east Asia, use the pitfall method to capture their prey. The pitchers that give the plants their name are made up of modified leaves, varying in shape and size. Some resemble narrow flutes, others bulging flagons.

All have the same objective – to lure insect prey using sweet-smelling nectar as bait. Insects are attracted by what seems like the promise of a meal and land on the lip of the pitcher. One false move and they slip into the vessel, whose wax-lined walls ensure that an insect cannot claw its way out. Its struggles to escape only stimulate glands in the pitcher walls, which secrete digestive acids that dissolve the victim in a matter of days.

The giant pitcher from Mount Kinabalu in Borneo has the largest trap – up to 40 cm tall and holding up to 4 litres of liquid. Large beetles, moths, butterflies and ants are often on this plant's menu, and it occasionally captures frogs, lizards and even small rodents. These larger animals probably slip in while pursuing insects.

The sundews, another carnivorous group, use a flypaper approach. Found in boggy regions all over the world, they supplement the minerals they draw from the nutrient-poor soil with an occasional insect meal. Sundew leaves are covered in fine hairs up to 1 cm long, the tip of each carrying a glistening, adhesive bead that mimics a drop of nectar. When an insect alights on the leaf, its feet get stuck and as it struggles to escape, it touches more hairs. The plant now senses a quarry, and nearby hairs – even if they have not been touched – begin to move towards the insect, which is soon entangled in a group of hairs.

The Venus flytrap – a close relative of the sundews from an area of coastline in North and South Carolina, USA – has a trap, also composed of modified leaves, with two lobes splaying outwards from a central midrib. Each lobe is fringed with a line of claw-like spikes. When open, the trap reveals its inner reddish colour, which makes it look like dead meat, attracting flies; nectar held in glands beneath the spikes is another lure. To reach either bait, the insects must crawl across the leaves, which are primed with sensitive bristles.

A single touch of a bristle does not spell disaster for the fly. The trap will shut only if that hair or another is touched within 20 seconds of the first touch. In this way, the trap avoids

HUNGRY PITCHER *Mosquito larvae are among the few creatures able to profit from Borneo's giant pitcher plant (left). They live in the pitcher, sharing the feast of trapped animals, without being consumed themselves. A wasp (inset) has fallen prey to a North American purple pitcher plant.*

BIT OF A MOUTHFUL Sundews catch their prey with sticky-tipped hairs. Small insects are soon overwhelmed by the hairs, which grip them tightly, although larger creatures, such as this frog, can usually escape the plant's clutches.

triggering itself if, say, brushed by a twig moving in the wind. Once sprung, the trap snaps shut in 0.3 seconds. Small insects such as ants can sometimes escape between the spikes, but for a larger insect there is no way out – its struggles make the plant squeeze shut even harder. Soon the two lobes are locked together and the cavity is flooded with digestive juices. The jaws do not reopen for about ten days, by which time the plant will have digested its captive. Ease of cultivation and the plant's fascinating eating habits have combined to make the Venus flytrap a popular houseplant.

Death chambers

The corkscrew plants of the genus *Genlisea* catch animals that live in the soil. Above ground, a corkscrew plant produces delicate, colourful flowers at the end of a long stem growing from a rosette of leaves. Beneath the soil, it has long, slender structures that probe in all directions. White and looking much like roots, these are, in fact, modified leaves, designed to trap and ingest microscopic soil-dwelling creatures, called protozoa. Each long, hollow leaf

divides into two twisted strands in an inverted Y-shape. Attracted to a chemical secreted by the plant, protozoa swim up these corkscrew arms until, just above the fork of the 'Y', they reach a swelling, called the bulb or bladder. Prevented from retracing their route by hairs on the inside of the leaf arms, the protozoa follow a one-way journey into the bulb, where they are digested.

The *Genlisea* plants belong to the same family as the bladderworts, rootless wetland species that operate the most complicated traps of all carnivorous plants. They get their name from the thousands of small bladder-like traps attached to their long, branching submerged stems. About the size of a pinhead but large enough to capture prey, such as mosquito larvae, a bladderwort's trap is triggered by touch and works by suction. Inside each bladder, glands absorb water and create a partial vacuum. The trapdoor, which hangs down from a hinge, rather like a garage door, is fringed with bristles. When a larva touches one of the sensitive bristles, the door moves ajar and, due to the vacuum inside, the trap sucks water in, carrying the larva with it. In one swift movement, the water swirls back to shut the door and the prey is trapped. Now the walls of the bladder begin to secrete digestive juices as the plant absorbs the food, while other glands suck out the water that came in with it. Within two hours, the bladderwort's trap has reset itself and is ready for another meal.

PLANTS IN THE DARK

A WHITE, GHOSTLY SHAPE APPEARS IN THE DARKNESS. A litter of pine leaves and twigs covers the forest floor, but apart from that there are few other signs of life in the remote depths of the coniferous forests spreading along North America's north-western coast. Examined more closely, the 'apparition' proves to be a plant with long, spindly stems, about 20 cm tall, each topped with a drooping, bell-shaped waxy flower. Known by two names, Indian pipe and ghost flower, the plant owes the former name to its shape, which resembles one of the clay peace pipes traditionally smoked by Native North Americans; ghost flower speaks for itself. With no chlorophyll whatsoever and with leaves reduced to small waxy scales up the stem, this anaemic growth looks more like a toadstool than a

plant. It cannot make its own food and must steal what it needs – not from other plants, as most parasitic plants do, but from a type of soil-dwelling fungus.

These 'friendly' fungi, called mycorrhizal fungi, are essential to the forest's welfare. While leafy plants are rare on the forest floor, the soil beneath is thriving with life where the threads, or hyphae, of the fungi form dense tangled masses. Lying just a few centimetres beneath the surface, they attach themselves to the root systems of trees, striking up mutually beneficial, symbiotic relationships with them. In return for sugars from the partner plant, the fungi act as an extended root network, increasing the surface area through which water can be absorbed by up to 100 times. They also break down certain nutrients, such as phosphorus, that are otherwise inaccessible to trees.

Mycorrhizal fungi are not confined to North America. Thousands of different types exist in all kinds of habitat across the globe – around 90 per cent of plants worldwide are estimated to have fungi partners. In certain regions, such as the tropical rain forests where the soil is very poor, plants could not live without the fungi, as they would not be able to obtain enough nutrients from the soil by their roots alone.

Like these other plants, Indian pipe plants engage in a relationship with mycorrhizal fungi – but this is no partnership. Instead, Indian pipe exploits the fungi's habit of bonding to the roots of several trees at once. By mimicking the roots of a tree, the plant tricks a fungus into attaching itself to its system. Now linked to numerous trees via the fungus's underground network of threads, the Indian pipe can draw off all the sustenance it needs, using the fungus as a go-between, even though it gives neither the fungus nor the trees anything in return.

Orchid spectre

Another 'ghost' plant, the ghost orchid, spends most of its life underground. Native to Europe, it is one of Britain's rarest plants, found in just a handful of locations and often disappearing for

RARE SIGHT The ghost orchid grows in a handful of locations in Britain. Bumblebees are attracted to the pale flowers, which smell rather like bananas.

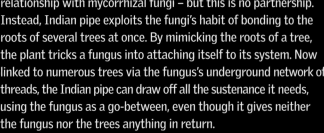

long enough to be declared extinct – only to reappear once more. It lacks leaves or proper roots, existing only as a branching underground stem, or rhizome, linked to a mycorrhizal fungus in a one-way relationship like that of the Indian pipe plant. After several years below ground, one wet spring the plant sends up an almost transparent, pinkish flower stem about 15 cm tall. This holds several delicate flowers with yellow petals, pinkish lips and a scent reminiscent of bananas. The ghost orchid seldom seeds naturally in the wild, reproducing mainly by means of buds on its underground stems.

In western parts of Australia, the underground orchid, *Rhizanthella gardneri*, is even rarer and more reclusive than the ghost orchid, with a fully subterranean life cycle. Only when it flowers does it offer a slight chance of being spotted above ground. At the start of the autumn rains, the orchid produces a tulip-shaped structure containing a cluster of more than 100 tiny maroon-coloured blooms. Exuding a musky odour that attracts insect pollinators, most notably termites, these flower heads are pushed up towards the surface, sometimes lifting the soil slightly.

The underground orchid is thought to be associated with a shrub called broombush (*Melaleuca uncinata*), because this plant is often found growing nearby. It probably hooks into a mycorrhizal fungus – one that is associated with the roots of the honey broom. Discovered as recently as 1928, the Western Australian underground orchid has an eastern relative, *Rhizanthella slateri*, found three years later some 240 km north of Sydney. It is not yet known which mycorrhizal fungus this species parasitises.

Direct action

Whereas Indian pipe and the ghost and underground orchids parasitise mycorrhizal fungi, indirectly taking nutrients from surrounding plants, the broomrapes plumb directly into the roots of other plants. There are more than 100 species of broomrape, found all over the world, and because they siphon off water and minerals, they can be serious pests to crops, such as sunflower, alfalfa, oilseed rape and various vegetables, by stunting the crops' growth. Underground dwellers once again, the broomrapes emerge only to put out peculiar-looking flowering stems, which lack chlorophyll and often appear brownish or yellowish.

TURNING HEADS The eerie white flowers of Indian pipe plants turn upwards when pollinated, revealing a central stigma with a ring of yellow stamens round it. After pollination, the whole stem gradually turns black.

GOING
GROWTH

FOR 3

GROWTH IS A RISKY BUSINESS. ONCE A PLANT HAS SENT OUT NEW SHOOTS, THERE IS NO TURNING BACK. Far from leading a passive existence, plants are constantly interacting with and responding to their environment. They move towards light and are aware of factors such as time, starting germination and subsequent periods of activity with great accuracy. Many plants – such as these rain-forest ferns in Puerto Rico – form partnerships with soil-borne fungi and bacteria. The way plants grow also reflects their habitats. On the cold, rocky slopes of California's White Mountains, bristlecone pines live a long, slow existence spanning thousands of years, while down in the Mojave Desert farther south wildflowers race through their brief life cycles, sprouting with the spring rains, blossoming and setting seed, all in a matter of weeks.

SMALL BEGINNINGS

AN ACORN WEIGHS JUST A FEW GRAMS, BUT IN TIME IT MAY GROW INTO AN OAK TREE WEIGHING MORE THAN 20 TONNES. The seeds of California's redwood trees are even smaller – about 3 mm across – yet they grow up to be the tallest and heaviest living things on Earth.

The incredible transformation is achieved by cell division – put simply, the process by which one plant cell divides and becomes two cells, which then divide to become four cells and so on. But for this process to begin in the first place, a seed must germinate.

Triggering germination

Whether carried on the wind or consumed by an animal, seeds end up travelling some distance from the parent plant. This enables plants to spread into new areas, yet it is something over which the parent plant has little control. Seeds may land on a perfect piece of ground, with plenty of light and nutrient-rich soil, or they may fall on sterile rock or into a lake. Because of this uncertainty, seeds are designed to wait in a state of dormancy until conditions become favourable to germination. To protect their softer parts during a wait that may last months or even years, most seeds have a tough outer case. This layer can be hard like a grape pip, or leathery like the coating on a bean.

Various triggers bring seeds to life. Most germinate when the

FROM LITTLE ACORNS Oak trees produce their fruits, acorns, in summer. Consisting of a seed wrapped in a tough protective coat, the acorns ripen during the autumn and are often dispersed by jays or squirrels, which bury them for winter food, then frequently forget about them. The abandoned acorns germinate into saplings, which grow into oaks that produce more acorns.

temperature and moisture of the soil reach the right levels for optimal growth, but some species have extra requirements. The seeds of the mesquite plant of south-western North America cannot germinate unless they have travelled through the gut of an animal, which roughs up the outer casing enough for the young plant to break through. Others, such as Australia's river red gum, need a period of flooding to wake them up, while some rock roses (*Cistus* species) respond to fire.

Touch and go

When first dispersed, seeds generally contain little water – just enough to keep the embryo plant ticking over inside. When conditions are right for germination, the seed begins to let water in through a tiny hole in its outer coat, called the micropyle. As the seed swells and its contents hydrate, enzymes are activated that enable growth to begin.

Soon, the first root emerges through the micropyle, digging down into the soil in search of more water and nutrients. As it grows downwards, the root splits the seed coat. Germination and the production of this first root are fuelled by the seed's own store of starches, proteins and fats, which likewise power the emergence of the plant's first shoot. When this happens and the shoot breaks through the surface of the soil, it opens out its first leaves. The plant is now ready to grow in earnest, creating its own food through the process of photosynthesis.

Taking the plunge and germinating is a risky business for a seed, since there is no going back once started. Each seed is minimally packaged – it stores just enough food to get its first leaves above the ground. If the seed has misjudged the triggers, it may find that it has emerged in the wrong season with too little light or water for it to survive. Alternatively, if it is buried too deep in the soil, it may not have enough energy to reach the surface of the ground. On the other hand, if the seedling has timed it right – and been lucky enough to land in a good spot – it will continue to grow up and out, feeding on sunlight and on nutrients taken from the ground by its developing root system.

Plant cell growth

Growth is a result of cell division. All plants are composed of cells, tiny structures made up of a cell wall enclosing numerous small bodies, or organelles, floating in a jelly-like fluid called cytoplasm. Chief among these small bodies is the nucleus, the cell's control centre, which contains the plant's DNA and organises the various activities within the cell, including growth. The largest of the organelles – occupying up to 90 per cent of the available space in a mature cell – is the vacuole, a bubble-like sac containing sap. Around the cell is rigid cell wall and

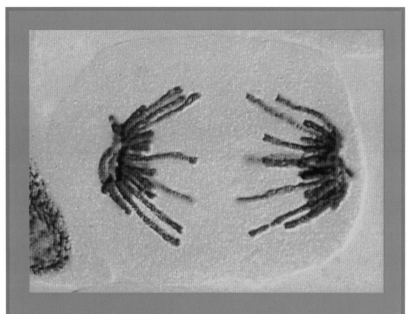

THE STAGES OF MITOSIS – CELL DIVISION
Mitosis is the process of cell division by which plants grow. It takes place in four basic stages:
1. Inside the cell nucleus, the cell's DNA stored in the form of thread-like chromosones replicates itself, resulting in two identical batches of DNA.
2. The boundary of the nucleus breaks down, allowing the two batches of DNA to move to opposite ends of the cell (above).
3. A cell plate forms down the middle of the cell, dividing it in two.
4. The plant builds a cell wall around each half-cell to create two new cells, each containing its own nucleus.

a thin layer of pectin (a kind of carbohydrate), called the middle lamella, which acts like cement in a building, attaching the cell to the ones around it.

Cell division, which takes place during a process called mitosis (see box, above), occurs in regions of active growth in the plant, known as meristems (from Greek *meristos*, meaning divided or divisible). Apical meristems, found at the tips of the plant's shoots and roots, produce vertical growth (upwards and downwards), while lateral meristems produce secondary (outward) growth. An example of secondary growth takes place in woody plants in the cambium layer (see pages 21–22), which runs the length of the stem and branches. Cell division in the cambium layer increases the girth of the plant, most spectacularly in trees. Secondary growth also occurs in the cork cambium, the first layer in from the bark, and produces the bark.

The exponential nature of cell division could, in theory, lead to unrestricted growth. In reality, factors such as a plant's genetic make-up and the amount of water, nutrients and sunlight available impose a limit.

> **If the seedling has timed it right – and been lucky enough to land in a good spot – it will continue to grow up and out, feeding on sunlight and on nutrients taken from the ground by its developing root system.**

SUBTLE STRENGTH

NEWLY GERMINATED SEEDLINGS ARE AMONG THE MOST FRAGILE OF LIVING THINGS. Yet, as they get bigger, they can develop extraordinary strength – enough to lift paving stones or burst through tarmac. These displays of power do not come about through sudden acts of violence. They are the gradual result of a combination of three factors: the uptake of water, the remarkable strength of cell walls and the division of cells as the plant grows.

Absorbing water – imbibition and osmosis

Water is taken into plant cells in two ways. Imbibition – from the Latin *imbibere*, to drink in – is a passive process by which plant matter (alive or dead) soaks up water, swelling to several times its original size. It works at the molecular level. A water molecule (H_2O) is made up of two hydrogen atoms and one oxygen atom and carries an electrical charge. The atoms in the tissues of plants also carry electrical charges, which attract the water molecules, causing them to enter the plant tissues. Here, the water molecules form strong chemical bonds with the atoms in the plant tissues. Since water molecules are also attracted to one another, they drag in more water behind them. As more and more water is drawn into the plant by imbibition, the tissues swell.

Osmosis is the process by which water is drawn into cells. The water moves from a region of low sugar concentration outside the cell to one of high sugar concentration inside the cell's vacuole (see page 55). Inside the wall of each cell is a membrane that lets in small molecules, such as water, oxygen and carbon dioxide, while preventing larger molecules, such as

sugars and starches, from exiting. Thus by osmosis, water continues to enter through the membrane until the cell is full and its walls begin to bulge. The cell is said to be 'turgid' at this point. The 'turgor pressure' of countless turgid cells not only helps to maintain a plant's rigidity, but also contributes to its feats of strength. This is also why plants wilt if their water supply is cut off – without water to plump them up, plant cells cannot maintain their rigidity, and they eventually collapse.

The miracle of cellulose

Plants grow in a particular direction because of the structure of their cell walls. The main component within a cell wall – accounting for much of its strength – is cellulose, a complex carbohydrate made up of long chains of glucose molecules. The cellulose forms bundles of fibres, called microfibrils. Along the sides of the cell, the microfibrils run parallel to one another, while at either end they are arranged in a criss-cross pattern, looking rather like woven cloth when viewed under the microscope. As the cell increases in size due to the uptake of water, the parallel bundles along the sides become elastic and stretchy, enabling the cell to enlarge along its

FACTS **THE CELLULOSE MICROFIBRILS IN PLANT CELL WALLS ARE** just a few nanometres wide, but weight for weight they have a similar tensile strength to steel. The strongest plant material in the world – with even greater tensile strength than steel – is bamboo, a type of grass.

98 PER CENT of the trunk and branches in a living tree are made up of dead cells.

PLANT CELLS USUALLY TAKE ABOUT 24 HOURS TO divide, but division can occur in just 8 hours. **FACTS**

length, while the criss-cross latticeworks at either end of the cell prevent it from getting any wider.

When plant cells reach maturity, they lay down secondary deposits of cellulose on the inner surface of the cell wall, forming a secondary wall. Among the strands of cellulose in this secondary wall, the plant also deposits a woody, hardening substance called lignin, which imparts even greater strength to the cell wall. Although the cells are now incredibly strong, they are no longer elastic along their length and so cannot grow any larger, but the plant can still make new cells in the areas of growth called meristems (see page 55). The relentless cell division combines with the internal pressure in each cell – maintained by uptake of water and strong cell walls – to create a virtually unstoppable force. Slowly, almost imperceptibly, a plant's roots and shoots can literally break through concrete.

STEADY PRESSURE A germinating bean pushes a rock aside as it emerges from the soil. It does this by applying pressure in steady increments, rather like slowly jacking up a car.

TOP GEAR

PLANTS THAT LIVE IN HARSH ENVIRONMENTS SOMETIMES GROW JUST A FEW MILLIMETRES A YEAR, but where conditions are good, plants can grow with great speed.

In temperate parts of the world, plants go into overdrive every spring, transforming the dull winter landscape into a world of green. In the tropics, where there is plenty of daylight, warmth and moisture all year round, it is not unusual for plants to grow several metres in a single month.

How well a plant grows depends on how well it is adapted to the living conditions it finds itself in, including the amount of sunlight it receives. While most plants thrive in full sunlight, a few prefer some shade. If light-lovers are overshadowed, they will still grow, but not to their full potential. Shade-lovers will do poorly in full sunshine. The type of soil and climate are also important, which is why experienced gardeners always find out where a plant grows naturally in the wild, so that these conditions can be re-created as far as possible in the garden.

Racing to the top

Most shrubs have a particular shape and height that they reach on maturity. Other plants – notably, the climbers – have no such constraints and are notorious for going on the rampage. Unlike a shrub, a climber is untrammelled by a static woody frame. Its long, flexible stems will keep on growing as long as conditions of sunlight and climate remain in the plant's favour and it has access to nutrients.

Virginia creeper, a woody deciduous vine from North America, can cover the wall of an average two-storey house in five years, ultimately reaching a height and

BARNSTORMER The various species of clematis are among the most familiar climbing plants to British gardeners. The plant collector, E.H. ('Chinese') Wilson brought back this fast-growing variety, Clematis montana var. rubens, from an expedition to central China at the start of the 20th century.

TENDRIL TOES The sucker pads of a Virginia creeper (Parthenocissus quinquefolia) grip a limestone wall. Whereas clematis climbs by coiling leaf stalks around some kind of supporting structure, Virginia creeper puts out tendrils that stick fast.

width of 15 m x 9 m or more. It climbs by means of tiny, round sucker pads at the end of branched tendrils, which in its natural forest environment enable it to scramble fast to the crown of a mature tree. The advantage of using Virginia creeper as a wall covering is that its suckers do not penetrate mortar, unlike the pervasive rootlets of ivy. Like all the vines, Virginia creeper tends to shade out any plant it uses as a support. In autumn, it produces a spectacular display of fiery orange and red foliage.

The 'scramblers', such as the mile-a-minute vine from eastern Asia, are also lethal to their supporting plants. Difficult to control and often regarded by gardeners as weeds, scramblers swarm over anything in their path, shutting out supporting plants from the sunlight and so preventing photosynthesis – as a result, the supporting plants frequently die back. The mile-a-minute vine

A climber's long, flexible stems will keep on growing as long as conditions of sunlight and climate remain in the plant's favour and it has access to nutrients.

(*Fallopia baldschuanica*) prefers to be in full sunlight and, in its efforts to reach the light, uses curved barbs along its stems to climb up and over other plants. The vine's common name is appropriate, if not precisely accurate – it can put on up to 15 cm of growth in a day. In the growing season, the mile-a-minute has reddish stems and distinctive light green triangular-shaped leaves. The plant is self-pollinating (see page 95) and produces large quantities of seeds, which can persist in the ground for up to seven years. Birds help the mile-a-minute to spread by feeding on its dark berries in autumn and passing the seeds in their droppings. Ants may also assist dispersal by carrying off seeds from beneath the parent plant.

Bamboos and stranglers

In the tropics, plants have all the requirements for lush growth, and tropical regions are home to some of the fastest-growing

plants in the world – above all, the bamboos, members of the grass family native to Asia and Africa. The largest bamboos can increase in height by 1 m per day (see opposite).

Another tropical group of speedy growers are the figs. The hundreds of *Ficus* species include the various strangler figs, whose aggressive and unusual growth strategy ensures their success in the rain forest. A strangler fig starts life as a seed nestling in the crook of a tall tree, growing slowly at first, since it does not have access to much light. It lives as an epiphyte (see pages 44–45), gleaning what nutrients it can from the debris that falls into the crook where it is lodged and absorbing any water that runs down the trunk of its host.

At the same time, the strangler fig is sending out lots of thin roots in the direction of the forest floor. When the roots meet the ground and tap into the water and nutrients available there, the fig begins a massive spurt of growth. From its crook in the tree, it sets off on a race to the top of the canopy, where its leaves can make full use of the light. As it grows higher, the fig encircles its host with a network of roots and stems so that it looks as though it is strangling the tree.

The fig is, indeed, murdering its host, but through starvation rather than by suffocation. By growing rapidly, bushing out and soaking up all available light, the crown of the fig puts the leaves of the host tree in the shade, preventing photosynthesis. Its roots are also taking most of the nutrients and water from the ground. In the end, the host tree dies, by which time the strangler fig has formed an extensive woody latticework around it, strong enough to hold the tree carcass in position. The dead host gradually rots away, providing the fig with more nutrients, and eventually vanishes, leaving a hollow cylinder of strangler fig where it once stood.

Speedy trees

Trees tend to grow to a pre-set limit in terms of size – they have a certain lifespan and do not go on forever – but some are more prolific in their growth rate than others. *Paulownia elongata*, native to China, is believed to be the world's fastest-growing deciduous tree. If conditions are sunny, powering photosynthesis in huge leaves that measure 75 cm across, the tree can reach a height of 4 m in its first year of growth. After that, *Paulownia elongata* grows at a more sedate rate of around 2 m a year, reaching a final height of 20 m.

An infamous evergreen 'sprinter' is *Cupressus leylandii*, a hybrid of two cypresses native to western North America. Not only is *Cupressus leylandii* one of the fastest-growing evergreens, it also attains an enormous size. *Leylandii* trees push upwards at a rate of up to 1.2 m a year and can reach a mature height of 30 m. When these trees are planted in closely spaced rows, their branches form a thick evergreen canopy that can plunge a garden into darkness, whatever the time of day. In Britain, a law has existed since 2005, which obliges gardeners to restrict their *leylandii* hedges to a maximum height of 2 m if a neighbour complains.

Certain vigorous growers are cultivated as fuel. Prompted by the 1970s' oil crisis, scientists started looking for alternatives to fossil fuels, studying many tree species and assessing their reliability as fast growers and high yielders of timber. In the UK, the two top species were varieties of poplar and willow. Although there are trees that grow more quickly, poplars and willows send up several shoots per plant, producing the best crop of timber per hectare of land. They are also the most reliable species for the British climate. To gain the maximum yield in the shortest time, short rotation coppicing is used. Cuttings of poplar or willow, measuring about 20 cm long and 1 cm thick, are placed in the ground, usually sprouting several shoots, which are then left to grow. Within just three years, they may be as much as 8 m high, and can grow even taller in warmer climates. The stems are harvested in winter by cutting them down almost to ground level (coppicing), and a fresh crop then grows from the base, which has a useful life of up to 30 years.

Besides being cultivated for fuel, fast-growing trees are a source of pulp for paper. Eucalyptus species put on about a metre a year and most mature into some of the tallest trees in the world. They do best in warm, dry climates and are grown for pulpwood in South America, Spain and Portugal, as well as their native Australia.

FAST-GROWING PLANTS

Many of the fastest-growing plants are climbers, but there are also speedy trees and grasses. Growth rates are for plants in Europe.

NAME (Scientific name)	GROWTH RATE
Russian vine (*Fallopia baldschuanica*)	Can grow up to 5 m in one season, and cover an area of 15 x 15 m in five years
Sweet pea (*Lathyrus odoratus*)	Can easily cover a 2 m tall arbour in a season
Ivy (*Hedera helix*)	Can cover an area of 10 x 5 m in five years
Common honeysuckle (*Lonicera periclymenum*)	Can cover 2 x 2 m in five years and grow up to 3.5 m tall
Periwinkle (*Vinca major*)	Spreads rapidly, sending out roots where stems touch the ground
Trailing bellflower (*Campanula poscharskyana*)	Spreads over and through other plants, ranging over several metres in a season
Lupin tree (*Lupinus arboreus*)	Grows 1.5 m in the first year and up to 2.5 m in five years
Blackberry (*Rubus fruticosus*)	Spreads roughly 2 m in each direction every year
Giant rhubarb (*Gunnera manicata*)	Each year produces new clusters of leaves measuring 4 m across
Elephant grass (*Miscanthus x giganteus*)	Easily reaches 4 m high in the UK after two growing seasons

THREE SPECIES OF GIANT

BAMBOO CAN GROW UP TO A METRE DAY – ALMOST FAST ENOUGH TO SEE. Although bigger than many trees, these giant bamboos – *Phyllostachys edulis*, *Gigantochloa verticillata* and *Dendrocalamus giganteus* – are grasses, producing shoots, or canes, that can be more than 25 m high and 30 cm in diameter. The giant species are native to China and south-eastern Asia.

Unlike tree trunks, bamboo canes do not increase in width as they grow. Young shoots emerging from a plant's underground stem (rhizome) have the same diameter they will have for the rest of their lives. But as a bamboo clump matures, it produces thicker and taller canes until, after about three years, full-sized canes begin to appear, such as these huge specimens growing in the Tamur Valley of eastern Nepal (left). Mature bamboo canes that are being grown for human use are left to harden for another three years, after which they are harvested by slicing them off near the base, in much the same way that a farmer might cut hay. Canes regenerate repeatedly from the base for up to 100 years.

Hollow bamboo poles are an excellent material for building houses, fences and scaffolding. Straight, light and easy to work, bamboo is extremely tough – ten times stronger than most woods – as well as relatively quick and easy to grow. In Costa Rica, one 60-hectare bamboo plantation produces enough material to build 1000 houses every year. Bamboo stems are also used for making paper. New shoots can be eaten, and bamboo is reputed to have medicinal uses, including the treatment of asthma and chest complaints. Bamboo sap is said to reduce fever. The many virtues of bamboo have earned it the titles 'friend of the people' in China and 'wood of the poor' in India.

GIANT BAMBOO

VITAL STATISTICS

CLASS: Liliopsida
ORDER: Cyperales
SPECIES: *Phyllostachys edulis*, *Gigantochloa verticillata* and *Dendrocalamus giganteus*
DISTRIBUTION: Bamboos, including smaller species, are native throughout tropical and temperate Asia and Africa
KEY FEATURE: It is the world's fastest-growing plant species

NATURE'S POWERS

FUNGUS-DEPENDENT As with other orchids, Goodyera repens *(or creeping lady's tresses) needs mycorrhizal fungi for its seeds to germinate. Once germinated, the mature plant can photosynthesise and provide for itself.*

PRIVATE PARTNERS

VERY FEW PLANTS ARE ABLE TO GROW ENTIRELY ON THEIR OWN. The majority – around 90 per cent – require at least some help from friendly soil-borne fungi known as mycorrhizas (literally 'fungus roots'). The long, thin threads of these fungi strike up associations with the roots of plants (see pages 50–51), sometimes forming a jacket around the root tips and sometimes actually penetrating the cells. Both plant and mycorrhizal fungus benefit, the fungus providing nutrients and water in return for sugars from the plant.

The degree to which plants depend on mycorrhizal fungi varies, but orchids rely on them totally – at least at the beginning of their lives – because without their fungus partners they cannot germinate. Whereas most seeds carry food reserves to fuel the plant's early days, the minuscule seeds of orchids contain just an embryo and must lie dormant until the creeping threads, or hyphae, of its fungal ally worm their way into the seed case. The hyphae go on to penetrate the cells of the embryo plant, forming coiled structures, called pelotons, which provide the carbohydrates that enable germination to take place. Soon, a shoot emerges from the top of the seed case. The beginnings of genuine roots also sprout, and the fungus migrates to these for the rest of the orchid's life, forming pelotons within the root cells. Of the millions of seeds each orchid casts to the wind, only the few that come into contact with the right mycorrhizal fungi survive. For some, the species of fungus is crucial, while others are less fussy and can pair up with a variety of fungi.

In the case of orchids, the exact relationship between plant and fungus is not entirely clear. The fungi provide carbohydrates for the orchids, but the fungi do not seem to benefit, certainly not initially, and it is unclear what prompts them to penetrate orchid seeds in the first place. As many as 15 years may pass before an orchid emerges above ground as a fully formed plant, and for all this time it relies on the benevolence of the fungus. In some cases the fungus can turn hostile, destroying the orchid, but mostly the plant appears to be in charge, controlling the level of infiltration and consuming the fungus as it wishes. When an orchid grows leaves and begins to photosynthesise, it may become independent of its partner, but some orchids remain partially or wholly dependent on fungi for their entire lives.

> **As many as 15 years may pass before an orchid emerges above ground as a fully formed plant, and for all this time it relies on the benevolence of mycorrhizal fungi.**

The nitrogen fixers

In another partnership – this time between plants and bacteria – nitrogen from the air is converted into a form that plants can absorb and use. Nearly 80 per cent of the air we breathe is made up of nitrogen, but this takes the form of N_2 gas, which cannot be used by most living things because of the strong bond that exists between the two nitrogen atoms. With the assistance of soil-living bacteria, certain plants can dissolve this bond and turn the N_2 gas into ammonia (a compound of nitrogen and hydrogen) or nitrate (nitrogen and oxygen). This is an essential process because all living things require nitrogen as a component of proteins and DNA.

The best-known example of this partnership is between bacteria called rhizobia (singular: rhizobium) and the members of the bean family – the legumes, which also include peas and clovers. Different species of bacteria are associated with different legumes, and when a rhizobium meets a likely legume root, it sends out chemical signals to check that it has found the right partner. Receptors on the cells of the legume roots are tuned to signals from a specific type of bacterium. If there is a match, the bacteria are allowed to enter the root, tunnelling into its middle by means of an 'infection thread'. Once deep in the root, the infection thread ruptures, depositing the bacteria, which multiply rapidly inside little pockets, or nodules, formed around them by the root. When the nodules are almost full, nitrogen fixation – the conversion of N_2 gas into usable nutrients – begins.

The plant's role is to supply the large quantities of energy, in the form of sugars and starches, needed to fuel the process.

The bacteria produce the ammonia, which the plant transports to the places where it is needed within its tissues. As a result, legumes are particularly rich in nitrogen compounds. When they rot down, they enrich nutrient-poor soil and are also excellent sources of nitrogen for herbivorous animals – and by extension for predators further up the food chain. Nitrogen is a key ingredient of protein, which is why legume seeds, which we harvest and call pulses, are particularly rich in protein.

Another plant group, the cycads, have a nitrogen-fixing relationship with cyanobacteria, a type of bacterium that contains chlorophyll and is able to photosynthesise. The cycads – which look like ferns or palms, although they are not related – are remnants of a group of plants that go back 200 million years to the time of the dinosaurs. They harbour colonies of cyanobacteria on modified roots, known as coralloids (because they resemble coral), which poke above the ground instead of growing into the soil. Whereas free-living cyanobacteria gain energy through photosynthesis, those in partnership with cycads rely on their hosts to provide their energy needs. In return for food and a place to grow, the bacteria convert nitrogen in the air into nitrogen-containing nutrients, which they pass on to the cycad. This relationship allows cycads to grow in places, such as semi-desert terrain, where there is little if any available nitrogen in the soil.

FRIENDLY INFECTION Peas are among the plants that benefit from a partnership with nitrogen-fixing bacteria, operating in nodules on their roots (below).

SENSING SUPPORT Climbers like this white bryony send out coiled tendrils with touch-sensitive tips. Once a tendril makes contact with a suitable support, it curls around it.

PLANT
SENSES

HEADS UP The narcissus is a short-day plant. When days start to lengthen in spring, it gets ready to bloom, opening its flower in a matter of hours in warm, sunny weather. It will not blossom in summer when the days are long.

EVEN THOUGH PLANTS HAVE NEITHER EYES NOR EARS, THEY CAN SENSE THE WORLD AROUND THEM AND INTERACT WITH IT. They can perceive light and grow towards it. They know night from day and one season from another. And they respond to touch, some more dramatically than others. All these sensory abilities are needed for survival.

The ability to move towards the light is fundamental to plant growth. Plants need light to power photosynthesis to make their food, and they seek it constantly, craning their stems around so that the leaves are exposed to sunshine. Growth hormones, called auxins, allow plants to do this. Gathering in the side of a stem that faces away from the light, auxins encourage the cells on that side to elongate and multiply, while cells on the sunlit side grow more slowly. As a result, the plant bends towards the light.

In temperate zones, plants are alert to the progression of the seasons, using cues such as changes in daylength and soil temperature to determine when to begin growing after the winter and when to flower. Daylength, or more accurately the length of the night, is the most important factor governing when plants flower. Some plants (long-day plants) flower only in summer when the nights are short and the day is long, while others (short-day plants) flower in spring or autumn when the nights are longer. These preferences explain why short-day plants, such as chrysanthemums, often do not flower indoors. Exposed to artificial light during the evening, they are under the impression that they are still in the long days of summer – and do not bloom.

Plants also always know which way up they are. The roots sense gravity and always grow down. This was tested in the zero gravity of space, where roots became confused and ended up growing in a disorderly way. According to one theory, plant orientation is decided by starch particles, which under gravity fall to the lowest point in each cell, indicating which way is down.

Flowers that tell the time

On a day-to-day basis, plants use an internal 'clock'. All living things, including humans, have internal clocks that coordinate various biological processes. In the case of plants, activities such as the closing of stomata at night are based on a circadian rhythm (a daily cycle – from the Latin *circa dies*, 'about a day').

This cycle was noticed by the 18th-century botanist Carolus Linnaeus, who observed that the flowers of some plants opened and closed at set times of the day. The four o'clock plant (*Mirabilis jalapa*), for example, opens its flowers each day at around 4 pm. Numerous other flowers are regular in their opening and closing, which enabled Linnaeus to devise a 'flower clock', with each flower planted in a sector matched to an hour on the dial. Experiments in which plants have been left in constant darkness confirm that the cycle is not dependent on sunlight but is controlled by an internal rhythm. Even so, after a few days without light, the rhythm begins to go awry, suggesting that plants also need the regular pattern of night and day to keep their internal clocks on time.

Besides shutting their flowers, plants can also close their leaves in response sometimes to an internal rhythm, sometimes to external stimuli. Among the prayer plants – so named because their leaves press together at night like hands in prayer – the action is believed to be a strategy to reduce water loss over night. Leaf closure, governed by the plant's internal clock, begins towards evening and takes a couple of hours to complete. The sensitive plant (*Mimosa pudica*) can move with lightning speed in response to touch. Common throughout the tropics, it has compound leaves made up of numerous leaflets, which close in a matter of seconds at the first nibble of an insect. At the base of each leaflet are pairs of cells plump with fluid. When fully turgid, the cells hold the leaflets in an open position. If the plant is touched, the lower cells in each pair release their fluid into the upper ones and become limp. The plant needs about 20 minutes to recharge its cells and open out the leaves again.

Since plants can respond to stimuli and sometimes react with startling speed, might they also be able to communicate with each other? Several experiments have shown that damaged plants release chemicals into the air warning neighbours to prepare their defences against attack. In some experiments, the plants seemed to be able to discern whether the damage done to their neighbour was accidental or caused by insects. This transfer of information appears to be a one-way process and so cannot be properly called communication.

FLOWER CLOCK

Swedish botanist Carolus Linnaeus noted that some flowers open and close so regularly that a range of plants laid out in order could work like a clock. Night-opening flowers tend to be pollinated by moths.

TIME	FLOWER
0500	Morning glory, wild roses
0600	Spotted cat's ear, catmint
0700	African marigold, orange hawkweed, dandelions
0800	Mouse-ear hawkweed, African daisies
0900	Field marigold, gentians; prickly sowthistle closes
1000	Helichrysum, Californian poppy; common nipplewort closes
1100	Star of Bethlehem
1200	Passionflower, goatsbeard; morning glory closes
1300	Chiding pink closes
1400	Scarlet pimpernel closes
1500	Hawkbit closes
1600	Four o'clock plant; small bindweed and Californian poppy close
1700	White water lily closes
1800	Evening primrose (below), moonflower
1900	Icelandic poppy closes
2000	Daylilies and dandelions close
2100	Flowering tobacco
2200	Night-blooming cereus (closes 0200)

FAST FORWARD

WHILE MANY TREES AND SHRUBS TAKE LIFE AT A LEISURELY PACE, OTHER PLANTS ARE IN A HURRY. Oak trees, for example, do not flower for their first 50 years, whereas annual plants germinate, grow, flower and set seed, all within a year or less. Typically, an annual wildflower germinates in the spring, then flowers and is pollinated in the summer, before dying back and casting to the wind the seeds that will produce a new generation the following year. These fast-track plants have some of the prettiest flowers – designed to attract insect pollinators

SECOND-SEASON SHOW Dark mullein is a biennial native to England and Wales. Its yellow blooms, with purple filaments, brighten up verges and hedgerows in the plant's second year of growth.

(see page 92) – among them blood-red field poppies, azure blue cornflowers and golden yellow marigolds. Many food crops are also annuals, including wheat, rice, maize and beans, their quick growth allowing us to harvest their seed each autumn.

Sprinting ahead

Desert annuals are in a particular hurry. Despite the name, they do not necessarily appear each year, since sporadic rainfall patterns often force their seeds to bide their time in a dormant state. But once triggered, these plants cram their whole life cycle into the space of a few weeks or less – the Sahara's *Boerhavia repens* speeds through its cycle in just eight days.

The blooming of desert ephemerals, as they are called, can be dramatic. In California each year, late February sees the start of 'desert watch', as people wait for a sudden explosion of plant life, which may occur at any time from then until mid-April. When this happens, the drab expanse of the Mojave Desert is transformed into a rainbow of colours, the intensity depending largely on the pattern of rainfall the previous winter, the arrival of warm spring temperatures and how long the dry soil has been waiting for a good drenching.

Desert ephemerals ignore small showers; their seeds wait for a downpour before they germinate, ensuring that they have enough moisture to race through their life cycle while the going is good. The best shows can be localised and short-lived – they may only happen in a particular area every four years or so and they may be over in a couple of weeks.

A biennial has a life cycle that straddles two years. Having spent the first year putting on growth in its leaves and storing food in its roots, the plant uses its food reserves to produce flowers and seeds in the following year, after which it dies. Familiar biennials include the foxglove, which produces a disappointing rosette of leaves in the first year but makes up for that with a spike of elegant tubular flowers in the second. Carrots, parsnips and beetroot are cultivated biennials – they are planted for their thick roots, which develop during the first year of growth.

FLASH FLOWERING Alpine plants, like their desert counterparts, live in harsh conditions. They must make the most of a brief flowering season, when they flood the mountain pastures with vibrant colours.

OLD-TIMERS

Individual aspen trees, their ghostly pale trunks towering 12–25 m into the air, live for only around 200 years, but the root system beneath survives through thick and thin.

ALL ONE A trembling aspen stand in the colours of autumn. Jettisoning their lower branches as they grow, aspens sprout slender branches near the top. These carry delicate, round leaves, which flutter and tremble in the slightest breeze, giving the trees their name.

A STAND OF TREMBLING ASPENS CAN, THEORETICALLY, LIVE FOR EVER. Aspen trees grow in magnificent, closely packed stands across North America, and the trees in each stand all sprout from the same root system, forming a single huge organism. This means that all of the trees in a stand are genetically identical – clones – each with the same pattern of branches and the same shade of bark. They even change the colour of their leaves in an identical way in autumn.

Individual trees, their ghostly pale trunks towering 12–25 m into the air, live for only around 200 years, but the root system beneath survives through thick and thin. Even if fire sweeps through a stand and the trees burn down, the organism as a whole lives on, regenerating from the roots. The only threat aspens face is that of being shaded out by thickly branched conifers, yet even if this happens it is usually just a blip in a stand's long life. While the individual trees die back and falter, the roots lie dormant in the ground waiting for a fire to come and destroy the conifers. As soon as this happens, the aspen roots send up fresh trees and the stand lives on.

Although trembling aspens can reproduce sexually (see page 95), for the most part they live and spread as clones. The success of this type of reproduction (called vegetative reproduction, see pages 90–91) means that aspen stands are commonly

10 000 years old. A stand known as Pando in Fish Lake National Forest, Utah, is the oldest-known aspen stand living today. Consisting of some 50 000 trees spread over 40 hectares, it is reckoned to be around 80 000 years old.

Tough customers

Even among plants that always reproduce sexually, a number of perennials can attain great ages and include some of the oldest living things on Earth. If the annuals and biennials are the sprinters of the plant kingdom, these perennials – usually woody plants, such as shrubs and trees – are its long-distance runners, growing and flowering year after year.

Oaks regularly reach ages of 400 years, and some are considerably older. Britain, which has the greatest number of ancient trees in Europe, possesses one of these venerable specimens: the Major Oak in the heart of Sherwood Forest in Nottinghamshire. With a circumference of 10 m, the Major Oak – named after Major Hayman Rooke, a local antiquarian who lived in the 18th century – is thought to be more than 800 years old, in which case it would have been a young tree when Magna Carta was signed. Time has taken its toll on the tree, which is now hollow at its base and relies on steel props to support its weightier lower branches, but its crown remains leafy and green.

Yews live even longer than oaks. Many British specimens, often found in country churchyards, are believed to be more than 1000 years old, and one of the oldest, the Fortingall Yew in Perthshire, may go back 3000 years. One reason for the yew's longevity is a remarkable ability to regenerate. The boughs of ancient, seemingly moribund trees sometimes put out aerial roots (see page 43) and grow a new 'trunk' within the confines of an old one that has lost its inner heartwood and become hollow. Alternatively, the branches may arch down to the ground and take root outside the old trunk, forming a circle of 'new' trees.

FACTS

THE OLDEST SURVIVING ELM TREES IN EUROPE ARE THOUGHT TO BE TWO 400-YEAR-OLD TREES, known as the Preston Twins, growing in Preston Park, Brighton. Dutch elm disease wiped out most of the world's mature elm trees in the 1970s, so the Preston Twins may be the oldest elms in the world, not just Europe.

OLIVE TREES GROWING IN THE EASTERN Spanish province of Castellón are thought be 2000 years old. Olive trees regularly live for 600 years.

A YOUNG ASPEN STAND MAY PUT OUT as many as 2.5 million shoots per hectare.

FACTS

CHURCHYARD TREE Yews are Europe's longest-living trees. In ancient times, they were regarded as sacred. Their toxic leaves may also have discouraged people from grazing livestock in burial grounds.

Because so many ancient yew trees are hollow, fixing their age is difficult. Without heartwood, the traditional method of estimating a tree's age by counting rings becomes impossible, so researchers use the great girth of yews to date the oldest specimens. Records of yew planting go back to around AD 900 in some places – because they are evergreen and reach such great ages, yews have been regarded as sacred since pre-Christian times, often seen as symbolic of regeneration and eternal life. By comparing the girth of a giant yew with the measurements of trees whose date of planting is known, scientists can reach a rough estimate of a tree's age. The Fortingall Yew's circumference can no longer be measured, because parts of its hollow trunk have disappeared, but in 1769 its girth was recorded at 17 m, which indicates a tree that was very old even then.

Growing high in the mountains of eastern California, many Great Basin bristlecone pines look more dead than alive, their trunks gnarled and twisted, ravaged by time and the elements until they resemble upright chunks of driftwood. These pines are thought to be the oldest living individual organisms on Earth (as opposed to clones, such as aspen stands). Bristlecones are easier to age than yews: by sampling and counting the rings in their trunks scientists have shown that they can live for more than 4000 years. At altitudes of more than 2500 m above sea level, the climate where bristlecones grow is cold and dry – in some years the land does not thaw. There may be just six weeks of warmth and, even in a good year, very little rainfall. As a consequence, bristlecones grow very slowly and are small compared to ancient oaks or yews. Even the most venerable specimens are no taller than about 12 m and have a maximum trunk diameter of 80 cm or so.

Hanging on

Among clone-forming plants, the trembling aspen's future seems assured, but another ancient species, King's lomatia, has been less successful. Just one clump of King's lomatia survives in south-western Tasmania; discovered in 1937 by a mining prospector called Charles Denison King, it is thought to be at least 43 600 years old. The clump amounts to 500 stems, which take the form of small, spindly trees, up to about 4 m tall, bearing shiny, prickly, toothed leaves. Unlike trembling aspen, which can reproduce sexually if need be, King's lomatia can spread only by producing clones. Genetically, it appears to carry three sets of chromosomes instead of two as most other plants do, making it a so-called triploid. Such plants are usually sterile, and so even though King's lomatia occasionally produces crimson flowers in January or February, no fruit or seed has ever been found.

Another clone-former, and possibly the longest-lived shrub, is the creosote bush, which ekes out an existence in the harsh, hot deserts of North America. Taking its name from the pungent smell it emits on the rare occasions when rain falls, this tough, bushy evergreen has small, waxy leaves to reduce water loss and can survive drought for up to two years. Like the trembling aspen, the creosote bush can reproduce sexually, putting out yellow flowers followed by fuzzy fruits containing seeds. Despite this, creosote bush seeds rarely germinate in the wild, so most reproduction is achieved by cloning.

Creosote bush clumps have an unusual circular growth pattern. They begin with a parent plant, which sprouts new plants from its roots. Growing up around the parent, these offspring plants also sprout new plants from their roots so the clump increases steadily in diameter. The stems in the centre of the clump die, causing the whole to take on the shape of a ring. Since the creosote bush grows slowly in its hot, dry environment, the process is very gradual, with individual plants living for 100–200 years and the diameter of the ring increasing by just 1 m every 500 years. Using this rate as a benchmark, scientists estimate that the oldest creosote clump in existence, King Clone in California's Mojave Desert, is more than 11 000 years old.

BRISTLECONE PINE

THE WORLD'S OLDEST TREE IS A GREAT

BASIN BRISTLECONE PINE IN THE WHITE MOUNTAINS OF EASTERN CALIFORNIA THOUGHT TO BE 4840 YEARS OLD – which means that it was a sapling when the ancient Egyptians were building the Pyramids. The exact location of this ancient survivor, named Methuselah, is kept secret, since the loss of an even older Great Basin bristlecone, known as Prometheus, in the 1960s. A PhD student cut Prometheus down so that he could study its growth rings as part of his research into climate change, in the process dating it precisely to 4844 years.

Various factors help the bristlecones to reach such great ages. Dense, resinous wood deters attack by insects, and the dry environment where they grow means that rot is rarely a problem. The trees can hold on to their needles for up to 40 years – much longer than other pines – which saves the energy other trees expend on replacing leaves. As the bristlecones grow older, some roots die back, along with the sections of trunk and branches above them – another energy-saving measure, as these parts of the tree no longer need to be fed nutrients.

VITAL STATISTICS

CLASS: Pinopsida
ORDER: Pinales
SPECIES: *Pinus longaeva*
HABITAT: Alpine
DISTRIBUTION: White
 Mountains, California
KEY FEATURE: Oldest living
 single organisms

PLANTS
ALL PLA

FOR CES

4

THE EARTH'S BIOSPHERE CAN BE DIVIDED INTO MAJOR ECOLOGICAL COMMUNITIES KNOWN AS BIOMES. These regions have similar geographic and climatic features and consequently characteristic communities of plants and animals. Plants help to define these biomes: from the Arctic tundra, where they must endure a bitterly cold, dry habitat with a growing season of less than 10 weeks, to deserts, where there are extremes of temperature and a scarcity of water. While some plants occupy a wide range of habitats, others are restricted to a particular biome, or even just one small part of a biome. This stately *Aloe pillansii* grows mainly in the intensely hot and arid regions of the Succulent Karoo, a biome of southern Africa that is home to the richest succulent flora in the world, with many species endemic to the area.

TEMPERATE LIVING

AUTUMN GLORY Before they drop their leaves, deciduous trees transport chlorophyll and other nutrients back into the body of the tree, turning the foliage into a blaze of colour.

BETWEEN THE POLAR REGIONS AND THE TROPICAL BELT LIES THE TEMPERATE ZONE, where plants experience varying lengths of day and seasonal temperatures. The most northerly latitudes – between 50° and 60° – are dominated by the biome known as boreal forest, or taiga, which runs in a belt through North America and Eurasia, including Canada, Alaska, Scandinavia and Siberia. With long, cold, dry winters, the trees that grow here are typically evergreen conifers, such as pine, fir and spruce, which are specially adapted to survive the snow and ice. The trees' branches slope downwards to help shed the snow load, and their needle-shaped leaves have a thick, waxy coating and sunken stomata to reduce water loss. Because the needles are retained all year round, photosynthesis can begin as soon as conditions are favourable, to make the most of a growing season that may be less than three months long.

Further south, the temperate deciduous and mixed deciduous and evergreen forests take over. These lie in a band roughly between 50° and 30° throughout Europe, north-eastern America and parts of eastern Asia, including China and Japan. (They also occur in the corresponding band in the southern hemisphere, in parts of Chile, south-eastern Australia and New Zealand.) In these regions there is a defined spring, summer, autumn and winter, and plants can enjoy a long growing season of six months. Instead of needles, the deciduous trees, which include oak, beech, maple and ash, make large flat leaves to maximise the absorption of summer sun. They drop these leaves as winter approaches when there is less daylight and temperatures plummet, often to below freezing.

In common with the evergreens, temperate deciduous trees produce overwintering or 'perennating' buds, which are formed during the growing season and encased in tough scales

WOODLAND LIFE Temperate deciduous woods support a variety of wildlife, including hedgehogs, which hibernate through the cold winter months. Plant-eaters that stay active during the winter feed on bark, berries and nuts.

to protect them in winter. Soft, pre-formed shoots beneath these scales wait until good growing conditions return, when they quickly burst into life and begin to photosynthesise. The temperate trees also share another feature with the evergreens: thick bark, which acts as insulation and prevents water loss.

Whereas evergreen conifers form a dense, year-round canopy that shades out the forest floor, deciduous forests have a thinner canopy allowing more daylight to filter down to the understorey where other plants can grow. In spring, the woodland floor bursts into life, as bulbs sprout and make use of the well-lit conditions beneath the still-leafless canopy. In the forests of North America, the three-leaved trilliums, with their three-petalled white flowers, cover the ground, while European woodlands are carpeted with bluebells and the tiny white flowers of wild garlic. Perennial plants, such as forest ferns, and the shrubby layer make use of the scanty canopy, too, producing flowers, setting seed and storing energy in their roots before the upper layer leafs over and light becomes more scarce.

Temperate grasslands

Where rainfall is too low to support trees but high enough to prevent desertification, grasslands predominate. They are mainly found in the interior of continents, where summers are usually dry and warm and the winters bitterly cold. The most extensive areas of temperate grassland are the prairies of North America, the pampas of South America and the steppes of central Europe, Russia and south-west Asia.

The soil in these flat, treeless expanses is fertile and nutrient-rich from the growth and decay of extensive root sytems of successive generations of grasses. Natural grasslands can be extremely rich in species. As well as grasses, there are also various sedges, wildflowers and shrubs. There are, for example, no less than 50 different species of plant growing in just one square metre of Russian meadow steppe.

OAK TREES OCCUPY A PROMINENT PLACE in temperate deciduous forests, from North America throughout Europe to Japan. In Europe, the most widespread species is the common oak, a large, long-lived tree that has been established for 10 000 years. Over time, many creatures have become adapted to live on and in it, so that it now provides food and refuge to more life than any other tree in Europe, from its roots to its broad canopy of leaves.

RED KITE This magnificent bird of prey builds its nest in the oak's main fork or crotch, or on a horizontal branch. Established pairs may use the same nest for many years. Old oaks provide nesting holes for birds such as pied flycatchers and redstarts.

GALLS Abnormal growths of a tree's tissue are produced by several types of insect, including midges, moths and, predominantly, wasps. Each of the brown pea-sized growths houses one or more of a wasp's developing larvae, and they can form on wood or leaves, and in buds. The largest galls, known as oak apples, measure 5 cm across.

STAG BEETLE Dead oak-tree stumps provide a home for stag-beetle larvae, which can spend up to seven years feeding on the rotting wood before reaching maturity. Other beetles, such as the deathwatch and the furniture beetle (better known as woodworm), lay their eggs in decaying wood, where the developing larvae soon chew tell-tale galleries of holes.

BLUE TIT Insect-eating birds like the blue tit hatch their broods to coincide with the spring flush of moth caterpillars that feed on oak leaves. The birds can be seen flitting through the canopy picking off the caterpillars and taking them to their young. Other insect-eating visitors include robins, wood warblers and chiffchaffs.

OAK BEAUTY Like many of the 200 species of moth that take up residency in oak trees, the oak beauty is perfectly camouflaged to perch on the greyish brown, deeply fissured bark. Other moths, such as the green silver-line, mimic the hue of oak leaves, while the buff-tip resembles a dead grey twig. The caterpillars of the green oak tortrix can be so abundant that they can defoliate an entire tree.

SQUIRREL The grey squirrel is one of many mammals that rely on the oak for food and refuge. It feeds on the autumn crop of acorns, often burying caches of them for later use. Deer are also partial to acorns, and they will browse on young shoots and leaves within reach during summer. Pipistrelle bats roost in hollow trees during the day, while the yellow-necked mouse and the common shrew may nest in the shrubby layer or in old birds' nests. Other mammals at home in oak woodland include badgers, moles, hedgehogs, voles and foxes.

YELLOWDROP MILK CAP
Several types of soil-borne fungi, such as yellowdrop milk caps, receive sugars and carbohydrates from an oak tree, while in return their networks of threads in the soil improve the tree's uptake of nutrients. Most of the time, the fungi remain below ground, but in the autumn their fruiting bodies – mushrooms and toadstools – appear on the forest floor.

HARDY EXISTENCE

WITH FREEZING TEMPERATURES, LOW RAINFALL AND FEW NUTRIENTS IN THE SOIL, the desolate, treeless expanse of tundra found at the high altitudes of the sub-Arctic – just south of the Arctic Circle – is one of the most inhospitable places on Earth. Add to the uncomfortable mix short summers of less than 10 weeks followed by the interminable dark days of winter, frost-laden winds, and a layer of permanently frozen ground (the permafrost), and you have a terrain suited to only the hardiest of plants.

The plants that do grow here tend to stay close to the ground, their prostrate woody stems keeping a low profile in the bleak ice-laden winds. All are dependent on a thin layer of topsoil just a few centimetres deep, which provides all the nutrients and almost all the moisture available. Conifers, such as the prostrate juniper, have needle-like leaves with the thick cuticles and sunken stomata typical of desert plants, and with the same purpose – to reduce water loss. There are also dwarf forms of willow, birch and alder, which, unlike their tall, temperate cousins, have stunted, gnarly growth and sometimes make do with just a single leaf per plant. The arctic willow, for example, creeps across the ground, its shabby-looking stems rarely growing more than 8 cm high.

Around 1700 different species of plant have found a foothold in this harsh terrain. Along with woody shrubs, such as *Dryas*, *Vaccinium* and *Empetrum*, there are grasses,

Beyond the tree line, even the wizened krummholtz trees give up the ghost and are replaced by low-growing hardy shrubs and by specialist high-altitude plants – the alpines.

ALPINE BEAUTY Edelweiss have taken root in a rocky crevice high above the tree line in Austria's Rofan Mountains.

sedges, mosses and lichens. Hundreds of specialist flowering plants provide a welcome splash of colour in the short summer. They include the yellow arctic poppies, which turn their heads to follow the course of the Sun, gaining as much warmth as possible, the purple-blue flower spikes of arctic lupins and the delicate white blooms of tufted saxifrage that stand 15 cm above a mat of fleshy leaves.

At more northerly latitudes, the soil becomes increasingly impoverished and plants need to be adept at taking up and using the scarce minerals available. They make tussocky or cushion-forming growth and are dotted over large stretches of bare ground. Clubmosses (*Lycopodium*) – descendants of the mighty prehistoric clubmosses (see page 20) – scramble over rocks on prostrate stems, rooting in the occasional patch of soil. Should a part of its stem die back, the plant withdraws any remaining minerals into its living tissue. *Lycopodium annotinum* thrives in this environment, forming extensive mats, each individual plant living for hundreds of years. Hardiest of all are the lichens, which colonise the thinnest of soils and even bare rock. They provide an important source of food for tundra herbivores, such as the caribou (or reindeer).

SUN WORSHIPPERS The heliotropic arctic poppy often grows in rocky terrain, where stones absorb heat from the Sun.

BRIEF EXPOSURE The upright catkins of arctic willow appear during the tundra's short summer.

The high life

Plants living at high altitudes experience many of the same problems as those growing in the tundra. Soil becomes increasingly poor and plants can experience sudden and significant changes in temperature, harsh winds and intense exposure to ultraviolet light.

As altitude increases, so the community of plants gradually changes, in much the same way as it does with increased latitude. In the foothills of the European Alps, for example, there may be mixed conifer and broadleaf woodlands, but higher up these give way to forests exclusively of conifers, trees better able to cope with the increasingly cold weather, exposed conditions and poorer soils that go with the territory.

Higher still, at the treeline, or timberline, the stunted trees known as 'krummholtz' – a German word meaning 'crooked wood' – prevail. Here the trees are definitely living outside their comfort zone. Wind-driven ice crystals blast down the mountainside, breaking off the vertically growing tips of trees and encouraging stunted and horizontal growth.

Beyond the treeline, even the wizened krummholtz trees give up the ghost and are replaced by low-growing hardy shrubs and by specialist high-altitude plants – the alpines. Because of the cold and wind, these perennial ground-cover plants keep low and grow very slowly. The winter fall of snow keeps them warm until the spring, when their colourful blooms cloak the moutainsides. Perhaps the best-known of all alpines is the edelweiss (meaning 'noble white' in German), whose delicate white, star-shaped flowers belie its ability to survive on inaccessible rocky peaks above 2000 m. A covering of fine hairs not only keeps the plant warm, but helps to protect it from the harmful UV rays that become more intense at high altitudes.

At the highest altitudes, beyond the shrubs and alpines, are rock-encrusting lichens. Even beyond the snowline there is life in the form of red algae, which stains the snow so that it looks like raspberry-ripple ice cream – a phenomenon known as watermelon snow.

THE MOST NORTHERLY GROWING TREE IS THE DAHURIAN LARCH.

Unlike most other conifers, this native of Siberia is deciduous. After winter temperatures of –50° C and below, springtime brings warmer air, but any moisture remains locked in the still frozen ground. By shedding its leaves until the thaw, the larch avoids losing water it cannot replace.

THE MOUNTAIN BUTTERCUP

grows at altitudes of 6500 m in the Himalayas.

THE TERM 'TUNDRA'

derives from a Lapp word meaning 'flat barren land'.

FACTS

DRY AND DUSTY

FEW PLANTS SUGGEST HEAT AND DUST LIKE THE CACTI OF NORTH AMERICA, and that familiar 'extra' of Hollywood westerns, the giant saguaro, is the most evocative of them all. With its distinctive arm-like branches and stems up to 50 cm across, this stately giant of the Sonoran Desert is supremely adapted to desert life. Like other succulents – which include cacti, aloe and agave – it takes up as much water as it can during the infrequent wet periods in order to sustain it during the long periods of drought. The water is stored in its barrel-like, ribbed stem. Its tissue swells until it consists of 98 per cent water, then slowly deflates as the liquid is used up. A thick waxy cuticle around the stem, and spines instead of leaves, help to reduce water loss. The spines also serve to shield the stem from direct sunlight and trap a layer of moist air – as well as forming a formidable barrier against grazing animals.

The succulents employ a special form of photosynthesis, called crassulacean acid metabolism, whereby they take up carbon dioxide at night and store it as malic acid in their tissues. During the day the plants convert this acid back into carbon dioxide, which they then use in photosynthesis in the normal way (see page 37). This adaptation means that they open their stomata only at night, instead of during the day when water loss would be greater, thus reducing water loss by 90 per cent. The downside to this method of photosynthesising is that plants grow at a much slower rate. A saguaro, for instance, will need to live for around half a century to get to a height of just 2 m.

The succulents do not tend to have deep root systems. When it rains they quickly grow a spreading network of temporary roots to soak up the water. These then shrivel up and die during the drought.

One drought-dodger that does put out long roots is the desert melon (*Citrullus colocynthis*), which grows in abundance in the Sahara. To get to the water table deep below the surface, it sends down taproots that can be up to 50 m long. The water is stored in large melon-like fruit, which resemble yellow cannonballs scattered on the desert sand. Mesquite and tamarisk are among other drought-tolerant plants that use far-reaching root systems to seek out water.

Many plants deal with drought by shutting down and sitting out the dry period in a state of suspended animation. Grasses and sedges wither and die off during drought, but beneath the soil their roots have energy stores that enable them to wait until the next rainfall when they spring back to life. Others store energy in giant tubers or bulbs. California's Cucamonga manroot, for example, stores its energy in a 100 kg tuber, while the sea squill (a native of the Mediterranean) develops a bulb the size of a football. These fleshy structures survive the hottest season buried underground, sending up leaves once again during milder, wetter times.

Perhaps one of the most extreme survival strategies is employed by the resurrection plant (*Selaginella lepidophylla*), which grows in dry soil and rocky outcrops in North America's Chihuahuan Desert. It cannot store water like its succulent neighbours, so in times of drought its rosette of thick, fleshy leaves curls up and becomes dry and brown. It can withstand almost complete desiccation, losing more than 76 per cent of its moisture (most plants would die after losing 12 per cent). The aptly named resurrection plant can remain in this dormant state for years and then when the rains do come, its cells rehydrate, so it appears to return from the dead.

FACTS

AROUND THREE-QUARTERS
of the world's desert lands have some form of vegetation. Only shifting sand dunes, where plants cannot anchor themselves, and certain parts of Chile's Atacama Desert, the driest place on Earth, are devoid of plant life.

THERE ARE AN ESTIMATED 1200 DIFFERENT SPECIES OF PLANT GROWING IN THE SAHARA DESERT.

A GIANT SAGUARO
can weigh around 6 tonnes – most of it water. It branches only when it reaches the age of 75, and can live for 200 years.

FACTS

SWEET BARREL Flowers bloom on a North American barrel cactus. The flesh of this tough desert-dweller is used in a range of confectionery called cactus candy, which has led to overharvesting of the plant which is now endangered.

WETLANDS

AQUATIC PLANTS ARE THOSE THAT HAVE ADAPTED TO WATERLOGGED CONDITIONS, colonising fresh and saltwater wetlands the world over. Some plants cope with seasonal flooding, as occurs in Botswana when annual rains swell the Okavango Delta into a beautiful oasis in the Kalahari, with pools and lagoons studded with water lilies. Others thrive in areas that are permanently flooded all year round, such as the extensive bogs, marshes and lakes of Biebrza Marshes in Poland. Where the sea meets the land there are plants that tolerate the salty or 'brackish' conditions and there are even plants that live beneath the sea in underwater meadows. Sometimes bizarre-looking landscapes form as in northern Canada where the larch-dominated swamps are known as 'drunken forests' on account of the way the trees lean and shift position in their unstable, waterlogged soil.

Water specialists

The feature all types of wetland have in common is waterlogged soil. The pockets of air normally found in soil are displaced with water, thus preventing oxygen from diffusing to the plant's roots. Ordinary land plants could not survive in such anaerobic conditions, but aquatic plants have adapted to cope. One widespread mechanism used by wetland plants is to extend the air spaces that naturally occur within the tissues of all plants so

that they reach down to the roots. The spongy stems then have a system of hollow 'pipes' through which air can pass to and fro, linking the roots to the ventilating pores (stomata) above ground. Some plants, such as the swamp cypress of the Florida Everglades and tropical mangrove trees, have special snorkel-like root extensions, called pneumatophores, which sit above the surface of the water or soil enabling the tree's roots to breathe.

Aquatic plants can be grouped into four types. The emergent plants, such as reeds and giant papyrus, live in shallow and slow-moving water. Their roots are bedded in the mud at the bottom of the water while their leafy parts 'emerge' above the surface and photosynthesise normally. Plants with surface-floating leaves like the water lilies also sink their roots in the bed of their habitat, but their long, flexible stems enable the leaves to float on the surface of the water. The leaves have air pockets to keep them buoyant and a waxy coating to keep water off their upper surface, where the stomata are located. The largest of the water lilies, the giant Amazon water lily, has leaves around 2 m across with upturned edges that push away competing plants until the waterway becomes a patchwork of giant lily leaves.

Free-floating plants, such as water hyacinths, floating ferns and duckweeds, drift on the surface of the water, their roots dangling below them adrift of the soil. Hairs on the roots increase the absorption of nutrients from the water.

FRAGILE BEAUTIES Like all aquatic plants,
water lilies (above and overleaf) are in danger
as wetlands become polluted or are drained.

The fourth type of aquatics are those that live entirely
underwater – the submerged plants. Rooted in the mud with
their leaves beneath the surface, they cannot photosynthesise
using carbon dioxide from the air but must absorb it from the
water. Many have specialised leaves that help to increase the
surface area available for absorption and photosynthesis. They
also help to minimise water resistance and thus potential
damage to the leaves. Some species, such as bladderwort,
supplement their diet by catching small aquatic insects.

Underwater meadows

Perhaps the most intriguing of the coastal plants are the sea
grasses. Although they look like grasses, with their long, thin
leaves, they are in fact flowering plants with the same basic
structure as land plants. They have stems, leaves and roots, and a
network of veins (a vascular system) for internal transport of
nutrients, but the difference is they spend their entire lives
submerged beneath the sea, anchored to the sea floor by their
thick, fibrous roots. They even flower underwater, the pollen
from male plants drifting through the water until it reaches the
stigma of a female plant.

Since they need sunlight to photosynthesise, sea grasses
tend to live in shallow, brightly lit waters in sheltered inlets and
bays, where they form thick 'meadows',
their green leaves swaying in the current.
Spongy air gaps in their tissues allow them
to transport oxygen down to their roots.
Australia has the greatest diversity, with
the biggest meadows forming an almost
continuous skirt stretching for some
1000 km along the west and south-west
coasts. Sea grasses play an important role
in the ecology of the fragile coastal zone,
helping to keep the water clear and
stabilising the sea floor by trapping
sediments in their roots.

SEA-FLOOR CARPET Sea grasses are a source
of food for many coastal sea creatures,
including the manatee. The thick growth also
harbours a variety of marine life, including
seahorses, sponges and molluscs.

WIDESPREAD AND RARE

WHILE SOME PLANTS GROW ONLY IN VERY RESTRICTED AREAS, others are globetrotters, colonising far and wide. The most widespread of all plants are the grasses. Barring certain desert regions, they grow all over the world, from the Arctic to the Antarctic. Some 9000 species of grass cover around 20 per cent of the Earth's land surface. The world's three most important food crops – wheat, maize and rice – are grasses, as are bamboos and reeds.

The mosses are another immensely successful group. Sphagnum moss, the main component of peat bogs, is alone thought to occupy 1 per cent of the Earth's surface. It copes with drought by storing a large amount of water in dead cells within its tissue. Others adopt the strategy of drying out and becoming dormant, then coming back to life with the first drop of rain.

Like mosses, the ferns were one of the earliest plant families (see pages 18–19) and throughout their long history they have adapted and prospered. The most prevalent is bracken, which, unlike most ferns, thrives in broad daylight, so is not restricted to the shady understorey of forests (although it resides there happily enough). The plant is drought-tolerant and grows in a variety of soils. Its leaves are also loaded with poisonous chemicals that keep herbivores away. With such an impressive armoury, bracken can outcompete grasses and spread prodigiously. Attempts by farmers to burn the invasive plant are thwarted by a final trick: it produces dormant buds beneath the soil on its rhizomes, which rise, phoenix-like, above ground.

Isolated communities

Endemic plants are those that live in only one specific place. The Galápagos Islands in the eastern Pacific, for example, are home

WETLAND GRASSES Reedbeds are an important habitat for a diverse range of wildlife, including this mute swan.

CREEPING CARPET Popular as turf in warm climates, Bermuda grass originated in Africa and is a resilient, fast-spreading species.

to a unique community of plants and animals. The life that exists there (at least before man arrived) found its way by being windblown, washed up by the sea or carried by birds. With Ecuador the nearest mainland some 970 km away, the islands' diverse plant life was left to evolve undisturbed for millions of years, resulting in around 180 endemic species. Among these are the six species of the Galápagos prickly pear cactus, which are low-growing and hairy where there are no lizards or tortoises to eat them, and upright and spiny where large reptiles are abundant. The largest of these cacti grow to 12 m, with trunks over a metre across.

In other parts of the world, species thought to be long-since extinct sometimes turn up unexpectedly. This happened in 1994, when a conifer believed extinct for 200 million years was discovered deep in a canyon in the Wollemi National Park, near Sydney, Australia. Seed from the wild stand was collected and propagated, and today specimens of the Wollemi pine, which resembles a monkey-puzzle tree and grows to 40 m, can be seen growing in parks around the world.

Sole survivors

In the Temperate House at Kew Gardens stands the world's loneliest tree. It is surrounded by other plants, yet none are of its kind. The cycad *Encephalartos woodii* is one of the world's rarest plants. Only one (male) specimen of *E. woodii* has ever been found in the wild, in South Africa, and one of its stems was brought to Kew in 1899. For the first time ever, in 2004, the cycad produced a large orange cone, but without a female plant there will never be seeds.

Although the cycads dominated the Earth 200 million years ago, just 250 species exist today and many of them are endangered. The reason for their decline stems partly from the fact that they are very slow-growing and very long-lived, factors that hinder their ability to adapt to changes in the environment. Because of their biology, cycads represent an important 'missing link' between the cone-bearing and flowering plants. Though cycads produce male and female cones, they enlist the services of insects to carry pollen from the male cones to the female cones, a method used by the flowering plants. Biologists strive to protect these 'living fossils' and there may even be a glimmer of hope for

E. woodii. It seems that on rare occasions, cycads have been known to change sex in the wild. It is a long shot, of course, but if botanists can find a way of changing the sex of one of the specimen's many offshoots, it might be possible to grow the tree a female partner.

On rugged Robinson Crusoe Island off the coast of Chile, the tree *Dendroseris neriifolia* is – like the castaway in Daniel Defoe's classic tale – another stranded survivor. There is just one single mature tree left, standing on a rocky outcrop at the eastern end of the island. A few saplings are being carefully cultivated, but the prospects do not look good. The island became a UNESCO World Biosphere in 1977 in recognition of the large number of endemic species, including 97 species of flowering plants. Even so, many of these plants face extinction, largely due to the voracious appetites of local wild goats and rabbits.

LOST WORLD Mount Roraima, a flat-topped tepui marking the border of Guyana, Venezuela and Brazil, boasts many unique plants, including Orectanthe septrum, *which grows in profusion in the harsh sandstone terrain. Mount Roraima was the inspiration behind Sir Arthur Conan Doyle's* The Lost World.

THE NEXT
GENERAT

5

ION

LIKE ALL LIVING THINGS, PLANTS PUT A GREAT DEAL OF ENERGY INTO ENSURING THE SUCCESS OF FOLLOWING GENERATIONS. One way of spreading is by putting out creeping stems, but this has a drawback – any new plants are genetically the same. Sexual reproduction ensures a good mix of genetic material, but for plants this, too, has a problem – they cannot move and so cannot get together to mate. Flowers deal with the problem. By attracting animals or catching the wind, they allow plants to swap pollen and make seeds. The seeds then have to be dispersed. Some plants, such as this common milkweed, give their seeds a feathery tip to catch a lift on the wind. Others encase the seeds in a sweet juicy fruit so that they will be eaten by animals and later deposited. And some arm their seedpods with prickles that snag the fur of passing animals.

ONE JUMP AHEAD

MANY PLANTS HAVE THE ABILITY TO TURN SMALL PARTS OF THEMSELVES INTO WHOLE NEW PLANTS. Called vegetative reproduction, it is an extremely effective way of spreading, in which plants display considerable ingenuity in getting the material into fresh ground away from the parent plant. Some grow elongated creeping stems; others shed baby plantlets from the edges of their leaves. Another mechanism is for a plant to 'hurl' parts of itself at passers-by, the fragments then hitching a lift as far as the inadvertent carrier will take them.

Not so cuddly

From a distance, the jumping cholla cactus of California's Mojave and Sonoran Deserts looks soft and furry, giving rise to its alternative name of teddy bear cactus. On closer inspection, its yellowish furry coat turns out to be a dense covering of prickly spines. The jumping cholla does not actually jump, but it sometimes appears to, growing in a series of cylindrical segments, which detach themselves at the slightest touch of a passing animal. Armed with their spines – each covered in barbs that lie flat against the spine on entering an animal's skin, but pull open when the spine is tugged at – the segments cling onto fur, skin or clothing. They fall off some distance away from the parent plant and, if the soil is suitable, put down roots and grow into new plants. Large stands of jumping cholla are often found to be genetically identical, since the plants all grew up from pieces that detached themselves from a single parent.

Many succulents can root from a single leaf. Since the leaves are fleshy and full of water, a detached one will survive for some time away from the parent plant and, if conditions are not too dry, develop into a new plant. The stonecrops are very successful at this method of vegetative growth, making them good ground-cover plants. Another group of succulents, from the genus *Kalanchoe*, has taken this method a step further, producing detachable ready-formed plantlets. The Mexican hat

READY TO DROP New plantlets cluster around the leaf edges of a Mexican hat plant, some of them already bearing roots.

THE HITCHER The jumping cholla's flowers are usually sterile. The plant spreads by detaching parts of itself onto passers-by.

DANGLING BABIES A spider plant sends out long stems with new plants at the tips, which will take root wherever they touch the ground.

AUTUMN SPLENDOUR *Brambles spread fast and can be almost impossible to eradicate from a patch of ground. A new plant may well grow up where the tip of this crimson-leaved cane touches the earth.*

plant, for example, produces miniature plantlets that fringe the edges of its leaves. When the plantlets have developed a few roots, they drop off to land on the soil below.

Another way of spreading is through modified stems in the form of rhizomes or stolons. Irises spread using rhizomes, thick fleshy horizontal stems found near or below the soil surface. As the rhizomes grow and spread, they may divide, producing a new set of roots, shoots and leaves. In time, the older part may die off so that the new shoots form separate plants. Stolons are long leafy stems that grow above ground, as in the wiry red runners of strawberries. New plants sprout from leaf nodes in the runners. Once one has taken root and started to grow, the stolon connecting it to its parent withers away.

Vegetative reproduction is so successful that some plants using it can become a nuisance. Wild bramble spreads by growing long stems, which rampage over fields and through woods and shroud abandoned buildings in tangles of thorny canes. The stems take two years to flower. In the first year, they keep growing through the summer. Then, in the autumn, a cane may take root where its tip touches the ground and a new plant will grow up from this point. In the second year, the stems that did not take root bear flowers and fruit before dying back. The bramble thus covers both bases: setting seed as well as sending out creeping stems, a combination that makes it supremely difficult to eradicate.

The walking fern also forms clumps, although it is not nearly as invasive as bramble. The plant takes its name from the way it appears to walk across the ground, rooting at the tips of its long, slender leaves. The leaf tips elongate and arch over, looking rather like stolons, then form new plants where they touch the ground. In time, walking fern forms dense colonies over moss-covered rocky outcrops, mainly in eastern North America.

FLOWER POWER

FLOWERS HAVE ONE PURPOSE – REPRODUCTION. They are a plant's sex organs, producing pollen (containing male sex cells) and ovules (female sex cells). Seeds are the 'offspring'. Although vegetative reproduction is successful with many plants, it has a major drawback – the plants all share the same genetic make-up. Sexual reproduction allows one plant to swap genes with another of the same species and leads to genetic variation. Being rooted in the ground, plants have the problem of getting the male and female sex cells together, and flowers are the solution. Over millions of years, a huge diversity of flower shapes and colours has developed with the aim of exploiting particular pollinators, including the wind, insects, birds, small mammals or lizards. Pollinators are like couriers, transferring the pollen from one flower to the female parts of another.

A flower's size, shape and colour indicate whether it is wind or animal-pollinated. Large, showy flowers signify an animal-pollinated plant; wind-pollinated flowers, including those of grasses and some trees, do not need to catch the eye of a pollinator and are barely noticeable at all – small and often green or brown. As the wind is rather erratic in its ability to deposit its cargo, wind-pollinated plants tend to produce large amounts of pollen. Their pollen-bearing stamens (see page 27) protrude from tiny flowers to ensure the pollen grains are launched on the breeze, while the (female) stigmas often have comb-shaped tips to catch the pollen as it drifts by.

For an insect's eyes only

Bees and other flying insects are the most significant animal pollinators, visiting a wide array of flowers to feast on their nectar and pollen, which is rich in fats and proteins. In a garden full of flowers, the insects are spoilt for choice, and each plant needs its flowers to be noticed – hence the great variety of flower colours, shapes and fragrances. Because insects see the world differently from, for example, humans, plants have designed their flowers appropriately. Insects cannot perceive the red end of the visible spectrum as clearly as we can and are not able to distinguish red from black. At the other end of the spectrum, the blue one, their eyes are much more sensitive than ours and can pick up ultraviolet markings normally invisible to human eyes. Looking at various flowers under ultraviolet light reveals them as an insect sees them.

BIG REWARDS Honey possums are tiny Australian marsupials that visit the flowers of a number of plants, including Banksia *(here).* Banksia *flowers offer pollen that is particularly rich in protein and plenty of nectar.*

Butterflies have an acute sense of smell, and a butterfly-pollinated flower will usually be scented, as in the strong sweet fragrance of freesias. Night-scented flowers, such as jasmine, attract the attention of moths. The Amazonian water lily uses its rich sweet perfume to attract beetle pollinators from far and wide. The large flowers open at dusk, and the scent attracts scarab beetles, which head for the heart of the blooms, where they find fleshy nodules, rich in sugar and starch. The beetles feast on them, unaware that as night falls the petals are closing around them. The next morning, the lily's anthers ripen and dust the inmates with pollen. By the evening, the flowers open up and release the beetles, which seek out the flowers of another lily plant, thus transferring the pollen.

What appears to us as a plain-coloured flower may carry a series of dashes, dots and other markings – a road map, directing the insect towards its sweet nectar reward.

Larger pollinators include bats (see pages 96–97) and birds, and once again plants have designed their flowers with these creatures in mind. Birds have almost no sense of smell, so flowers that rely on birds for pollination do not bother producing perfume. On the other hand, birds have excellent eyesight and an appreciation of colour, so the flowers that wish to attract their attention must be big and bright. They are usually red, as birds' eyes, like our own, are sensitive to this end of the spectrum.

Making colourful and fragranced flowers to attract pollinators takes a lot of energy from a plant, but there is a good reason for it. Although some flowering plants can self-pollinate (or will do so as a last resort), most prefer to cross-pollinate. In a genetically diverse population, when disease strikes, at least some individuals will survive; the plants will also be able to adapt gradually to different habitats.

SPECIAL DELIVERY

THE MICROSCOPIC WORLD OF POLLEN GRAINS IS ONE OF MARVELLOUS SHAPES AND INTRICATE PATTERNS. Each type of plant has its own design, sometimes a spiky sphere, sometimes a flat angular disc, sometimes triangular. All pollen grains are tough and built to last – they have to be since they will go on perilous journeys through the air or on the backs of animals to reach the heart of another flower.

Pollen is highly distinctive, and by examining it under a microscope, botanists can tell which plant or family of plants it came from. Although people tend to think of it as a yellow powder, pollen can be brown, orange, purple or black. A grain's outer walls may be pitted with pores and grooves, or spiky and rough, or perfectly smooth. The shape reflects its mode of transport. Pollen carried by animals is usually heavy – often spherical with spines to stick in fur – while wind-borne pollen needs to be light and aerodynamic, so it is often flat and angular.

Only a tiny proportion of pollen reaches the right destination. Wind-pollinated plants, such as grasses and some trees, produce the greatest amounts to ensure that at least some lands where it should. A single birch-tree catkin may contain 5.5 million grains – and each tree carries thousands of catkins. A lone ragweed may release up to a billion pollen grains. Plants that are animal-pollinated do not need to produce as much pollen, because there is a higher chance that their pollinators will transfer the pollen to another plant of the same species.

All about sex

Each pollen grain comprises two male sex cells encased in an outer wall. Made of sporopollenin, an incredibly tough material that is highly resistant to decay, the outer wall's job is to protect the contents of the grain, and it can endure for many thousands of years, even when its contents are long dead.

The male sex cells in one flower's pollen need to reach the female sex cells inside the ovules of another (see page 27). The ovules are usually found deep in the heart of the flower, connected to the outside via a tube, called the style, with a sticky, sensitive pad at its tip – the stigma. When a pollen grain lands on the stigma, it sends out biochemical messages, which signal to the stigma that it should allow the grain to grow a tube down the style to reach the ovules. The male sex cells travel down this tube and fertilise the egg cells inside the ovules. The process can happen in a few hours or over several months.

Since animal pollinators may visit several types of flower, pollen ending up on the stigma may come from a different plant species, but it will not fertilise the eggs. In this case, the pollen grain is the wrong shape and has the wrong biochemical markers, so nothing happens. Since many flowers contain both male and female parts, there is also a chance of self-fertilisation, but most plants have mechanisms to prevent this. In the most sophisticated,

GONE WITH THE WIND The wind blows tiny clouds of pollen from a pine flower. The pollen grains of many pines have air-filled bladders that help them to fly.

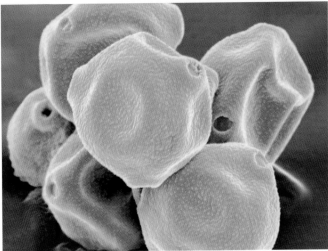

PURPOSE BUILT The pollen grains of a rose of Sharon flower (top) are typical of pollen that is transported by animals – relatively heavy and with a spiky or sticky surface. Wind-blown pollen, such as that of a birch tree (above), is lighter with angular surfaces.

the stigma recognises from the pollen grain's chemical signature that it has been self-produced and rejects it. Plants with this system are termed 'self-incompatible'. Other plants, including date palms, avoid self-pollination by separating the sexes – each plant has entirely male flowers or entirely female flowers. Another method is to make sure that the male parts of a flower mature well before its female parts are receptive.

Although most flowering plants do what they can to avoid self-pollination, some use it as a last resort. The highly successful weed, rosebay willowherb, operates this system. It tries to avoid self-pollination by separating the maturation of its anthers and stigmas by several hours, but if any flowers are left unpollinated, they shrink into themselves, pulling their stamens down so that the pollen-carrying anthers touch the stigmas. This enables self-fertilisation to take place. The plant will not have the benefits of genetic variety, but at least it will set seed. Self-pollination is preferable to no pollination at all.

PERFECT PARTNERS

MOST PLANTS ARE POLLINATED BY A VARIETY OF ANIMALS, BUT SOME ARE HIGHLY SELECTIVE, designing their flowers to be specially attractive to a particular type of insect, bird or mammal. Although the plants seem to be narrowing their chances by focusing on just one pollinator, at least that pollinator is assured. Through a process of co-evolution taking place over millions of years, the plant and pollinator reach a point where one may no longer be able to survive without the other.

In the Sonoran Desert of south-western North America, not much goes on during the heat of the day. But as the

FRUITS OF ITS LABOURS A lesser long-nosed bat swoops in to feed on the fruit of an organ pipe cactus. Earlier in the year, bats will have helped to pollinate the flower that has now set its seed.

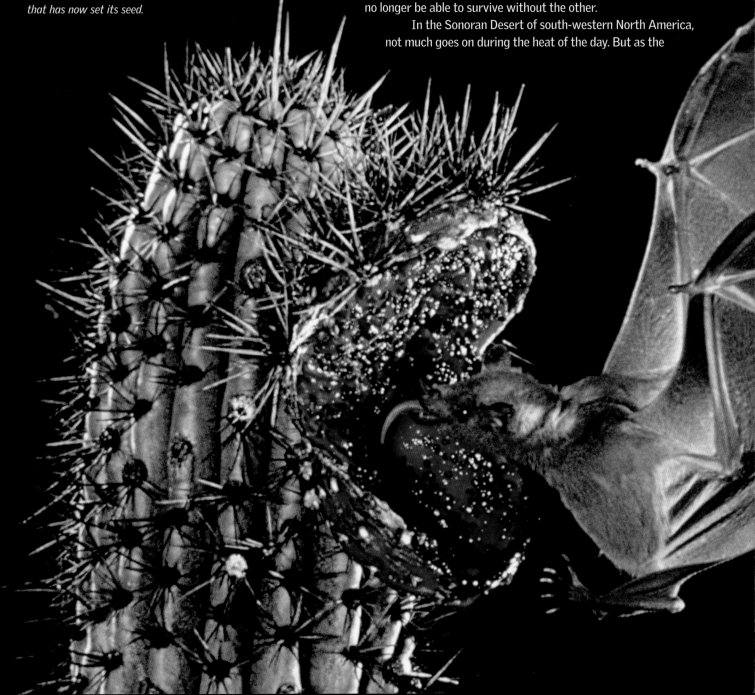

air cools at night, the desert residents set about their business. In summer, the nights are particularly active, as this is when lesser long-nosed bats are flying in on their yearly migration from Mexico. The bats are nectar-feeders in search of a meal – and the organ pipe cacti oblige them, timing their flowering season to coincide with the bats' northward journey. The cacti's flowers are designed to be bat-friendly – large and robust and conveniently open at night, when they emit a sweet, musky odour that the bats find irresistible. The flowers are white, so they are easy for the bats to see, and as a final allure, they offer the bats a drink of rich, sweet nectar. As they drink their fill, the bats reach down with their long tongues to the base of the tubular blooms and get a face full of pollen. When they move on to another flower, they transport the pollen with them.

The cactus is pollinated, and the bats have a further treat to look forward to. The plant now sets its seed, which it carries in a large, sweet fruit. Later in the summer, when the bats are preparing to go back south to their winter home in Mexico, they feast on the fruit, stocking up on vital calories. This time they have to share the bounty. Other mammals and birds feed on the pulp, swallowing the seeds, which travel through their guts to emerge in their droppings some distance from the parent cactus.

Another plant in the same deserts, the yucca, has formed a remarkable relationship with its sole pollinator – the yucca moth. The yucca forms rosettes of stiff, sharply pointed leaves, out of which a gigantic creamy white flower head emerges on a tall stem. Whereas most flowers are fertilised when a pollen grain lands on the tip of a sticky stigma, in yucca flowers several pollen grains have to be forced down inside the stigma before fertilisation can occur. This is where the yucca moth comes in. A female moth knows that she has to stuff the pollen down. It is hard to imagine how this behaviour arose, but the advantage for the moth is that it ensures that the flower will set seed, and the seed will provide food for her young.

After pushing down several bundles of pollen, the moth lays one or two eggs in the side of the flower's ovary at the base of the style. She gathers up some pollen from the flower's anthers, before heading off for a fresh flower to repeat the process. The moth larvae develop in safety inside the yucca's seedpod, eating some of the seeds before the seedpod dries out and breaks open. The remaining seeds empty out, and the larvae drop to the ground where they bury themselves in the soil and pupate.

CO-DEPENDANTS A female yucca moth stuffs pollen into the stigma of a yucca flower. The plant is pollinated and in return some of its seed provide the moth's larvae with food.

Sole mates

The partnership between the fig and the fig wasp has evolved to the point where the fig has turned its flowers inside out to provide a safe haven for its pollinator's grubs. At the same time, it has effectively isolated itself from the chance of being pollinated by any other insect.

The fig's flowers are held within small green spheres that hang in clusters from the main trunk. Each sphere holds thousands of tiny flowers, which are inaccessible except through one tiny opening. A female fig wasp squeezes through this hole, losing her wings as she goes, and enters the chamber inside, which is lined with the fig's flowers – male flowers near the entrance and female ones deeper inside. The female wasp carries pollen from another fig plant in her leg pouches, which she unpacks and spreads over the female flowers. In doing so, she fertilises the fig. Now she does something that seems detrimental to the fig's wellbeing. She begins to lay her eggs within the female flowers, piercing right through the stigma and style in a flower to reach its ovary. Several females may lay their eggs in the same fig and the result is hundreds of eggs laid in the flowers.

When the grubs hatch, they eat their fill of nutritious seeds, developing rapidly in the safety of the chamber. Adult males emerge first and seek out the females, mating with them as soon as they hatch. The males then chew out an escape route for the females. The females, which have been wandering around the chamber picking up pollen from the male flowers, fly off to a new fig and begin the cycle once more. Although many, if not most, of the fig's flowers will have been parasitised by the fig wasp, some will have survived and set seed – enough to allow the fig to continue. It seems the sacrifice is worthwhile.

SNEAKY TRICKS

THE RELATIONSHIP BETWEEN PLANTS AND THEIR POLLINATORS IS NOT ALWAYS STRAIGHTFORWARD. Over millions of years, reward systems have evolved, in which animals transport the pollen for particular plants in return for a drink of nectar, but in some cases one party tricks the other. Some animals break into flowers to steal their nectar without carrying out any pollinating duties, while some flowers trick animals with false promises of food or sex – although in a few instances, this deception seems to have worn thin.

Bending the rules

It is easy to see why the bee orchid is so named. At a casual glance, it looks as if a fat bumblebee has landed on a pink three-petalled flower. But look closer and the 'bumblebee' turns out to be part of the orchid's flower, and the pink petals are actually sepals (see page 27). The intricate patterning is part of an audacious con – to lure in male bees on the pretence of offering sex.

FADED ATTRACTION The flowers of a British bee orchid imitate female bees as a lure for male bees, even though the trickery no longer seems to work.

Widespread in Britain, the bee orchid is one of a group of orchid species (the *Ophrys* genus) found throughout Europe, all of which employ a similar ruse – making their flowers resemble the insects they hope to attract. The fly orchid, for example, mimics the female of its pollinating insect, the digger wasp, even producing a chemical that imitates the female's mating pheromone. Male wasps copulate with the fly orchid blooms, and as they do so they pick up pollen, which they transfer to the next flower they visit. Another species, the mirror orchid, has developed flowers that look remarkably like the females of a type of scoliid wasp. The flowers' blue petals resemble the female wasp's iridescent wings and are edged in a furry fringe much like the wasp's hairy abdomen. As a male wasp alights on a flower, gripping what it thinks is a female, its weight brings down the flower's anther, which neatly stamps pollen on the insect's head.

The trickery practised by *Ophrys* orchids can backfire. Botanists have observed that when disgruntled wasps or bees have been duped a few times, they learn to avoid the flowers of these orchids. In Britain, bee visitations to the bee orchid are incredibly rare. It is not known why this should be so. It could be that the orchid's true insect partner is now extinct, in which case it may be the beginning of the end for this particular species. For the time being, it survives by pollinating itself.

False food

Some flowers lure in insects with the promise of a meal. The carrion flowers are so named because they smell of rotting meat. The odour draws in beetles and flies from miles around, and to make their allure even more effective the carrion flowers do their best to look like dead meat as well as smell like it, with flesh-coloured petals covered in hairs.

In some instances, when a fooled insect crawls into a carrion flower, the flower traps it. In Europe, the Dutchman's pipe or birthwort imprisons its pollinators for several days. Gnats are drawn to its foul-smelling tubular flowers and slip down a wax-coated pipe into an inner chamber. Downward-pointing hairs prevent the insects from escaping by the way they came in and they remain in the chamber, where the flower feeds its hostages with rations of nectar, because it needs them to stay

alive. Then, after a few days, its anthers ripen and dust the gnats with pollen. The downward-pointing hairs now wither and the gnats can make their escape. The chances are that they will be lured into another Dutchman's pipe and pollinate it.

Carrion flowers also include one of the world's largest and most extraordinary flowers – that of the titan arum, which grows only in Sumatra. The titan arum's gigantic flower head (or spadix) may be 2.5 m tall and carries hundreds of male and female flowers around its base. The female flowers mature ahead of the male ones and when they do so, the spadix starts to give off a sickening smell, which calls in sweat bees. The bees, which may be dusted with pollen from visiting other flowers, wander over the female parts, depositing the pollen. After a day or two, the

BIRD BANDIT The purple-crowned fairy has a short beak that would not be able to reach the nectar deep inside a heliconia flower. It solves the problem by pecking a hole in the base.

male flowers ripen and, in their turn, deposit pollen on the bees, which then fly off to pollinate another flower. The impressive size of the titan arum serves to broadcast its scent across a huge area. It has to do this because other titan arum flowers are rare, and it needs to attract insects from great distances.

Nectar thieves

Some animals steal nectar from plants. A few types of bumblebee have become skilled burglars, piercing the bases of flowers for an easy drink. The species that do this tend to have short tongues, so by piercing the bases of long-fluted flowers, such as comfrey, they increase the number of flowers they can take nectar from. But although the bees get all the benefits of the energy-giving fluid, without even messing up their fur, all is not lost for the plant. The robber bees do not steal from every one of its flowers, so other pollinating insects continue to visit. Also, with some of the nectar stolen from a few of the plant's flowers, the insects will have to visit more flowers to get their fill. As a result, they may have to fly farther afield, and any pollen they pick up will travel a greater distance, leading to a greater degree of gene swapping.

Some birds, too, have learned to steal. The flowerpiercer hummingbird of the Andes lives up to its name by using a specialised beak with a hooked tip. It grabs the base of a flower with the beak so that it can pierce the flower and lap up the nectar. Another hummingbird, the purple-crowned fairy from Ecuador, pierces only larger flowers, such as heliconia. Because of its short beak, it would not be able to reach the nectar in these flowers in the usual way.

FINAL FLOURISH

HEADS ABOVE THE REST A flowering Puya raimondii *makes a striking feature within the stark landscape of the Andes. Each flower in the flower spike measures about 5 cm across.*

MOST LONG-LIVED PLANTS FLOWER EVERY YEAR, BUT A FEW OPT FOR A DIFFERENT STRATEGY. They grow slowly for many years, saving up their energy; then they stage one magnificent flower display, after which they die. Producing flowers, pollen and subsequently fruit takes a large amount of energy from a plant. Some, the annuals, grow, flower and set seed, all in the space of a few months – then they die, exhausted by their efforts. Long-lived plants go more slowly. The majority – the perennials – flower once or sometimes twice a year, pacing themselves in a natural cycle of growth and dormancy. Those that flower only once in a lifetime follow the same pattern as the annuals, except that it takes them years – in some cases 100 or more – before they are ready to produce their flowers. Like the annuals, these plants put everything into the flowers, usually held in large spikes or clusters and including some of the most dazzling floral displays in the plant kingdom. Then, like annuals, they set seed and die.

Andean blossoming

Living at altitudes of about 4000 m in the Bolivian and Peruvian Andes, *Puya raimondii* is one of the last group – it flowers just once in a lifetime. Although flowerings are rare events, the flowers when they come are hard to miss. The land here is dry and stony, and journeying through it travellers get used to the vast treeless landscape. Then suddenly, in the distance, a tall, thick 'trunk' may come into view, emerging from a spherical bush of spiky leaves. The unusual-looking plant is a bromeliad, a member of the same family as the pineapple as well as many of the epiphytes that perch on the branches of rain-forest trees. The 'trunk' is, in fact, a flower spike some 10 m tall – the tallest in the plant world – covered with flowers. Each spike holds thousands of creamy white blooms with orange anthers, packed around a woody stem.

A *Puya raimondii* lives for 150 years before it flowers and dies, a strategy that suits its harsh mountain lifestyle. In this cool, dry, high-altitude setting, the plant needs plenty of time to build up the necessary reserves to flower – by contrast, *Puya raimondii* grown at lower, warmer altitudes in the USA have flowered after just 30 years. It would be pointless to build up reserves, only to become food for a herbivore before reproducing, so any plant like this must have adequate defences against predation. *Puya raimondii* protects itself with stiff, sword-shaped leaves, edged in appetite-suppressing barbs. There are no animals in the region that would want to tackle it.

The agaves, a group of succulents that grow in desert regions across North and South America, share this once-in-a-lifetime flowering style. Because of the amount of time it takes them to bloom, they are sometimes known as century plants – something of an exaggeration, since they take anything between 5 and 50 years to flower, depending on the species and its growing conditions. The larger agave species produce tall flowering stems which, rather like those of *Puya raimondii*, come up out of a rosette of tough, sword-shaped leaves.

Tropical suicide pacts

Also in the Americas, rain forests between Costa Rica and Colombia have a large tree that flowers only once. Known as the suicide tree, it may take 100 years to reach maturity, developing large fin-like buttress roots to support its 50 m tall reddish brown trunk. As soon as the tree has flowered and set seed, it

Because of the amount of time it takes agaves to bloom, they are sometimes known as century plants – something of an exaggeration, since they take anything between 5 and 50 years to flower.

dies, falling limb by limb to the forest floor within about a year. Often, several trees in a population synchronise their flowering, then die together in what seems like a mass suicide pact. Such a life cycle is rare among trees and unheard of in temperate climates, but it has benefits in a tropical rain forest where plants compete vigorously for a share of sunlight. By flowering together, the trees ensure cross-fertilisation, and by dying soon after they have set seed, they create a gap in the canopy for their seedlings to grow into. Botanists have discovered that suicide trees flowering at the same time are usually genetically unrelated. This is important because it means that the plants ensure a good mixing of genetic material – but it has left botanists wondering how unrelated trees manage to synchronise their flowering so efficiently.

RARE FEAST Hummingbirds take advantage of the abundant nectar offered by agave flowers. The plant grows for up to 50 years before producing its towering flower heads.

STARTING LIFE

THE EFFORT THAT GOES INTO POLLINATION PRODUCES A VIABLE SEED, WHICH WILL THEN DEVELOP INTO A NEW PLANT. Contained in every seed is a complete embryo plant, together with enough food to keep the embryo alive for months or even years. In addition, to give seeds the best chance of survival and of being dispersed, they are often encased in sweet fleshy tissue (a fruit), which attracts the attention of animals. These feed on the fruit and help to distribute the seeds. Alternatively, some plants use wind to disperse their seeds or even employ catapults to send the seeds shooting skywards.

Seeds, pods and fruit

When a pollen grain lands on a compatible stigma, it grows a pollen tube, which pushes down into the flower's ovary and meets up with an ovule containing an egg cell. The pollen grain sends its two male sex cells (see page 95) down the tube, one of which unites with the egg cell and grows into an embryo plant. The second male cell combines with other cells in the ovule to form food-storage tissue, called endosperm, which accumulates starch and nutrients as the embryo develops. In some seeds, the endosperm is retained throughout the embryo plant's dormancy and subsequent germination to sustain it. A protective coat, called a testa, forms around the embryo, and the whole combination is called a seed.

Seeds remain inside the ovary. At first, they are too small to be seen, but gradually they grow larger and the ovary swells around them, forming a seedpod or fruit. At the same time, the petals of the flower may wither and drop. Over time, the seedpod or fruit gets bigger and bigger and the seeds inside it develop their hard coating.

Some seedpods become dry and brittle as they mature. These include the poppy seed capsule, which dries to a hard brown head perforated with small openings, rather like a pepper pot. The tiny black poppy seeds escape through the openings as the seed head rocks in the

To make sure that a fruit is not eaten before the seeds are fully mature, its fleshy coat remains full of sour-tasting sap while the seeds are developing. Animals, including humans, dislike the taste and will leave the fruit alone.

FERTILE FRUIT Only fertilised ovules develop into seeds. The seeds in this mature western peony pod (left) are black and shiny. The unfertilised ovules are red.

wind. In other dry pods that we know as nuts – as in hazelnuts and walnuts – the ovary wall becomes exceptionally dry and hard to protect the seed inside.

In most fruits, the ovary wall develops into a thick juicy flesh. Some fruits, such as peach, plum and cherry, contain a sweet layer of tissue around an inner stone, or pit, which protects the seed hidden inside it. Others, such as the passion fruit, contain numerous seeds, each with a sweet sticky covering, all held inside a thick skin. Strawberries present their many seeds on the outside of a sweet fleshy centre. A pineapple is not one fruit, but many fused together, each of which develops from a different flower on the pineapple's original flower head.

The different types of fruit derive from subtle differences in how they form, and botanists have several terms to describe them. These include drupes (such as peaches and plums, with a stone or pit inside), berries (such as grapes, in which the seeds and edible flesh develop from a single ovary) and pomes (such as apples and pears, in which the fleshy tissue develops not from the ovary wall, but from the base of the flower).

Ways of scattering

Once its seeds are mature, a plant needs to disperse them as widely as possible. If the seeds simply fell off the plant and landed beneath it, the subsequent seedling would be competing with the parent plant for light and resources. So plants aim to spread their seeds across a large area, and there are several different ways in which they do this.

One method is to encase the seeds in a delicious fruit, which means that an animal, such as a bird, is likely to eat it. In some cases, a bird may spit out the seed once it has removed the flesh around it. In others, it may consume the seed along with the flesh so that the seed passes through the bird's body, emerging unharmed as part of its droppings. It is quite common to see rowan saplings growing beneath a mature Scots pine, for example. A bird has fed on rowan berries, then sat in the branches of the Scots pine and passed out the rowan seeds. This is an ideal situation for the seed, which can germinate in a ready-made patch of manure some distance away from the parent plant.

To make sure that a fruit is not eaten before the seeds are fully mature, its fleshy coat remains full of sour-tasting sap while the seeds are developing. Animals, including humans, dislike the taste and will leave the fruit alone. As the fruit ripens, its flesh

becomes sweet and the plant signals this fact with a change of colour, usually from green to a shade of red, orange or purple.

Seeds germinate in various ways. Some do so as soon they hit the ground. Others have to go through a period of maturing while they sit on the soil. Rain and the elements, as well as soil fungi, get to work on the seed cases, eventually softening them enough for the plant embryos inside the seeds to start to grow. Some seeds will only germinate once they have passed through the gut of an animal. They need the acids of an animal's digestive system to break down, or scarify, the seed's toughened outer coat. In this way, the plant makes sure that the only seeds to germinate are ones that have travelled in the gut of an animal and are likely to have been deposited some distance away from the parent plant.

*DEVELOPING POD
Each seed inside a broom pod is attached to the ovary wall by a stalk, through which it receives the food it needs to grow. The pod swells as the seeds develop and eventually it dries out and releases the mature seeds.*

SEEDS ON THE MOVE

A SWEET-TASTING FLESHY COVERING IS NOT THE ONLY WAY TO ATTRACT THE HELP OF ANIMALS. Several plants native to the parched bush of South Africa coat their seeds in a thin oily skin that appeals to ants. An ant will often drag a seed back to its nest beneath the soil, where it strips off the coating and eats it, leaving the seed intact. By recruiting ants in this way, the plant reaps a double advantage. Not only have the ants carried the seed some distance from its parent plant, but they have also positioned it deep in the soil – the perfect place for germination. The seeds are also hidden from larger animals that might otherwise eat them.

Other plants, such as agrimony, lesser burdock and cocklebur, produce spiny, spiky fruits that catch a ride on passing animals. The hitchhikers are armed with hooks and barbs that grab hold of clothing and fur, sometimes embedding themselves so well that they are almost impossible to shake off. Animals such as foxes, sheep, dogs and horses cannot pick the burs out of their coats as humans can, so they have to find a handy branch or post where they can rub them off. For the burs and the seeds within them, this means they have a good chance of travelling some distance from the parent plant before being dislodged.

Some plants have taken the hitchhiking method to a rather painful extreme – getting a lift by literally penetrating their carriers. Native to South Africa, the grapple plant has seedpods that resemble instruments of torture and befit the plant's alternative name of devil's claw. Surrounding the central pod, and going off in several directions, are a series of long, stiff arms ending in sharp hooks. When a large animal, such as an elephant, treads on one, the hooks rip into the sole of its foot, firmly attaching the pod. This stays with the animal for several miles, often causing acute discomfort, until eventually the arm wears away and the pod drops off. Another plant found in South Africa, the devil thorn or stud plant, produces a hard fruit, shaped rather like a drawing pin, with a sharp central spike that easily pierces the feet or hoofs of passing mammals. As the seedpod is dragged around, it sheds its cargo of five seeds.

Going with the flow

Plants that live near waterways have a ready form of transport available to them. Their fruit or seeds may be brought down during storms and land in the water. They then travel wherever the current takes them, often to a convenient spot farther downriver, or in some cases across the ocean. In Europe, the alder, a familiar sight along riverbanks, disperses its seeds in this way. Alder seeds have wings, so they can be carried by the wind, but they also have pockets of air inside, so they can float. The seeds often begin their germination in the water, and by the time they wash up on a likely riverbank, they are ready to send down roots and grow.

In Central America, *Entada gigas,* a climbing plant that snakes through the canopy of Costa Rica's tropical rain forest, is another plant that uses water transport. Locally called the monkey ladder vine, since monkeys clamber up it to reach the higher parts of the forest canopy, it produces beautiful heart-shaped seeds, the size of the palm of a hand. These are known as sea hearts, and during rainstorms they wash into local rivers. *Entada gigas* is a legume (a member of the same family as peas and beans), and the seeds form in 2 m long dangling pods – the world's longest seedpods. Many of the seeds wash up on riverbanks, where they take root. Some reach the sea and travel many miles over the waves before drifting back onto the shore. Locals collect them and make them into pendants or lucky charms. Travelling from their Caribbean home on the Gulf Stream, sea hearts can sometimes end up on the beaches of Northern Europe.

Seeds designed to travel by sea are well prepared for their journey as

HANGERS ON Burdock burrs cling to the face and coat of a sheep. They will eventually work loose and fall out, by which time the seed will have been carried far from its source.

THE LARGEST SEED IN THE WORLD, THE COCO-DE-MER ('COCONUT OF THE SEA'), IS CONTAINED IN A FRUIT THAT WEIGHS UP TO 30 KG AND CAN MEASURE 50 CM ACROSS. Early European mariners first saw cocos-de-mer floating in the Indian Ocean, and for a long time their origin was a mystery, with some people believing that they came from a plant that lived at the bottom of the sea. In fact, the palms producing them grow in the Seychelles, which Europeans discovered in the 18th century. The giant coco-de-mer fruit is also known as the double coconut, because of its two lobes – a shape that is suggestive of the female pelvic region and has led to the fruit's reputation as a fertility symbol.

Coco-de-mer palms may take 25 years to produce flowers. A palm carries either male or female flowers – male flower spikes can be up to 1 m long. Once seed is set, a fruit stays on its tree for up to seven years before reaching maturity, slowly growing the thick husk that covers it when it finally falls to the ground or into the sea. When it reaches a suitable resting place, it may take another two years for its seed to germinate.

Rare and exotic, cocos-de-mer have always been collected. As well as being acquired as souvenirs and fertility symbols, they have been hollowed out into bowls and other ornaments, to the extent that the palms are now very limited in their range. Just two populations exist in the wild today – on the Seychelle islands of Praslin and Curieuse. The palm is classified as an endangered species and export of its seeds is strictly controlled. Licensed seeds sell for more than £300.

VITAL STATISTICS

CLASS: Liliopsida

ORDER: Arecales

SPECIES: *Lodoicea maldivica*

HABITAT: Tropical rain forest

DISTRIBUTION: Praslin and Curieuse in the Seychelle Islands

FEATURE: The largest seed in the world, each seed contained in a single fruit or nut

CO-CO-DE-MER

they have internal air cavities that make them buoyant and tough coats that are impervious to water. They are also equipped with large stores of food – as in the thick white flesh of coconuts – since they may be bobbing across the waves for several months. This mode of dispersal is not precise and – as with the sea hearts – the seeds of these tropical plants often turn up on more temperate shores, where they have little hope of germinating.

One of the longest-distance travellers among the sea drifters is the seed of the box fruit, which may be in the water for more than two years. The plant is native to Polynesia in the Pacific and its seeds, which are about 10 cm long, look like boxy, flat-sided coconuts. They are found washed up on beaches across the tropical Pacific, where they are often used as fishing floats.

Flying start

An alternative way to travel is by air. Plants may launch their seeds using natural catapults, hurling them anything between a few centimetres and 100 m away. The catapult mechanism relies on ingenious constructions in the seedpod and is usually powered by the sudden release of tension. Often, the seedpods have weak spots that suddenly rip apart as the pod dries out. Examples of such pods belong to the pea family, including the sweet pea and vetches. Other pods, including those of Himalayan balsam, need a trigger of some kind, such as an animal brushing past or a gust of wind.

Possibly the most impressive plant to use this form of dispersal is the dynamite tree, which grows throughout the tropical regions of North and South America. The trunk of the tall tree is armoured with tiny sharp spikes, but its most vicious weapon is its explosive seedpods. The dry, segmented fruit look like wooden tangerines and, when ripe, they explode noisily. The explosion scatters the numerous disc-shaped seeds as much as 100 m from the tree, and for anyone standing close by, the shrapnel – sharp segments from the ruptured pod – can cause serious injury.

Less dramatic than catapulted seeds, but just as effective in getting around, are the winged seeds of trees such as ash, field maple and sycamore. As the seeds become dislodged, they set sail through the air, spinning and twirling far from the parent tree. The wing slows the descent of the seed, so that it travels farther.

Some plants, such as honesty, give their seeds a flat papery seed case, which is easily lifted by the wind. Others have a fluffy parachute attached to each seed. The latter method of wind dispersal is used by some of the most successful weeds and pioneer plants, including dandelion, rosebay willowherb, thistle and ragwort. The seeds themselves are tiny and light, and the fluffy tip is lifted by the slightest breeze, as in a dandelion clock.

A few seeds, such as those of orchids, are so tiny that they can drift on the wind without the need for a parachute. In tropical rain forests, where many orchid species live as epiphytes perching on tall trees, the seeds are carried high on warm rising air currents. As a result, orchids are found throughout the rain forest's many levels of vegetation.

The waiting game

Seeds can remain dormant for centuries, like time capsules waiting until conditions are just right for germination. Timing is of the utmost importance, since each seed gets only one attempt to germinate. Seeds of the sacred lotus have been known to wait a thousand years. When seeds were removed from the bottom of a

FIRE ONE! Cranesbill forms a beak-shaped pointed pod with five segments. As the pod dries the segments curl up, projecting the seeds up to 3 m away from the plant.

DRIFT AWAY In South Africa, the light seeds of the conebush have fluffy parachutes. Equipped with these, they can float for many miles on the slightest breeze.

lake in China and germinated in a laboratory, radiocarbon-dating showed that they were some 1200 years old. There is circumstantial evidence of 10 000-year-old arctic lupin seeds germinating. Although the seeds were not carbon-dated, they were retrieved from a layer of tundra that dated back ten millennia.

Seedbanks make use of the longevity of seeds to store plants' genetic material for future use. Such repositories are useful when a plant species becomes extinct in the wild, or for breeding new crop varieties. With so many plants threatened by destruction of habitat, climate change, invasion of alien species and overexploitation, scientists want to preserve as many as possible. The Millennium Seedbank at Wakehurst Place, West Sussex, holds more than 18 000 species of wild plants and aims to have 24 200 by 2010. Among the seeds stored there are samples from all of the UK's 1400 native plants, including 300 endangered species.

TAILSPIN The winged seed of a Dipterocarp tree spins as it falls from the topmost canopy of a Borneo rain forest. The spinning slows it down so that it can travel farther on the wind.

When seeds arrive at the Millennium Seedbank, they are sorted and cleaned and then dried at temperatures of 15–18°C in dry air. This process takes about a month, after which the seeds are placed in airtight containers, ready for long-term storage in cold rooms kept at a temperature of –20°C. Every so often, a sample of seeds is removed from storage and germinated to check that the seeds are still viable. If stocks run low, seeds will be germinated and grown to produce a fresh batch for storage. In such conditions, seeds can live for hundreds of years and some species for thousands. Mung beans, for example, are thought to have the potential to survive for 24 000 years.

In February 2008, a giant 'doomsday' seedbank, which can store up to 4.5 million seed samples from all over the world, opened above the Arctic Circle. The Svalbard Global Seed Vault is a giant concrete box cut 100 m into the side of a mountain on the island of Spitsbergen, 1000 km south of the North Pole. The objective is to preserve seeds in case of ultimate disaster, such as global nuclear war or catastrophic climate change. Unlike the UK's Millennium Seedbank, the Svalbard bank stores seed from known crop varieties, rather than wild plants. Locked away in the chilly Arctic permafrost, the seeds will be stored at –18°C, and if the worst should happen, they will be available to replenish the world's crops from scratch.

ARMED
RESPONSE

6

FROM THE MOMENT LIFE BEGINS, PLANTS FACE A MULTITUDE OF HAZARDS – from the voracious appetites of insects and larger animals to the ravages of fire. Rooted to the spot and unable to run away, they have had to become skilled in self-defence. As a response to animal predators, some plants have developed physical barriers. California's jumping cholla cactus (left) has sharp spines instead of leaves to deter desert browsers from munching on its water-filled tissue. Other plants, such as the stinging nettle, are armed with chemical weapons – in some species, these are so potent they can kill. Plants also have ways of surviving natural events, such as flame-retardant sap to minimise damage by fire or adapting their growth in the face of howling winds. Even so, they are not immune to disaster – like all living things, plants can succumb to disease.

KEEP OUT

The thistle is a veritable fortress of prickles, which cover its stems and leaves, while needle-like bracts (modified leaves) encase the flowers. Not surprisingly, animals tend to avoid thistles when other food plants are available.

IN THEIR NATURAL ENVIRONMENTS, PLANTS LIVE IN CONSTANT DANGER. Tender, leafy shoots full of sugars are a tempting prospect for a number of creatures – from caterpillars to large herbivorous mammals. With no way of fleeing their enemies, plants have evolved an armoury of physical defences. Some even employ 'watchdogs'.

A few plants, such as the mulleins (*Verbascum* species, native to Europe and Asia), cover their leaves in a dense coat of hairs, called trichomes. Viewed under a microscope, these stiff, branching bristles look like trees in a miniature forest. Not only do they keep out sucking insects, such as aphids, which like to pierce the skin of leaves and suck out the sugars, they also deter fungal spores from taking hold and infiltrating the leaf tissue. Wild comfrey is another plant with hairy leaves. Also known as hound's tongue, because its texture is like the rough tongue of a dog, it has unbranched trichomes, which are stiff and sharp enough to deter soft-bodied caterpillars.

To ward off larger herbivores, such as cattle and deer, plants need more forceful deterrents. The thistle is a veritable fortress of prickles, which cover its stems and leaves, while needle-like bracts (modified leaves) encase the flowers. Not surprisingly, animals tend to avoid thistles when other food plants are available. Holly carries spines at the edges of its leaves, each major vein ending in a sharp point. Browsers leave holly alone to avoid hurting their mouths, while caterpillars find the leaves' thickened edges too tough for their jaws. Hawthorn, blackthorn and other similar shrubs have spikes – in fact, modified short branches – while the rattan palms of tropical rain forests have barbs along the length of their canes. These spines, which can be 30 cm long, emerge from leaf sheaths to protect the tender growing points within.

Juicy morsels in the desert

Cacti store water in their tissues to last them through dry times and so would seem like an obvious food choice for creatures, such as mule deer, living in the deserts of south-western North America. Yet thanks to some of the nastiest spines in the plant world,

PROTECTIVE COAT An impenetrable carpet of branching hairs covers a mullein leaf. Like a stab-proof vest, the mat prevents insects from piercing the tissue beneath.

THORNY PROBLEM The fearsome-looking white spines of many African acacia species are more flimsy than they seem, but they serve their purpose as a conspicuous deterrent to plant-eating animals.

makes matters worse, and for humans the most effective route to freedom is to 'wait a bit', then unhook oneself thorn by thorn. As with many other acacias of the African savannah, the wait-a-bit thorn's sharp spines are a deterrent against the region's numerous plant-eating animals. Acacia thorns tend to be effective against grazers, such as zebra and antelope, but giraffes are able to use their long prehensile tongues to get through the defences and reach the tender leaves beyond.

Sending in the troops

As its name suggests, the bull's horn acacia of South America has two-pronged thorns, resembling a bull's horns, but the plant does not rely solely on these barbs for its defence. If a leaf-eating insect alights on a branch, it will be met by the acacia's secret weapon – an army of stinging ants. The ants kill the marauding insect, and in return the plant gives them shelter inside its hollow thorns. The acacia also makes sure that its security force keeps fighting fit by providing the ants with food in the form of nectar exuded at the base of the thorns and orange nodules of protein and fat-rich tissue at the tips of the leaflets. The ants are very thorough caretakers – they also chew away plants that encroach upon their host's space and cut off any seedlings that sprout near its base.

Several acacia species employ ant watchdogs. In Africa, the whistling thorn hides biting ants in the bulbous bases of its large black thorns. To reach this refuge, the ants have to chew a doorway into the thorns, which then whistle when the wind blows across them. The ants kill insects and attack the sensitive mouthparts of larger browsers.

animals mostly leave cacti alone. The spines are the remnants of leaves, which means that in cacti, unlike most other plants, photosynthesis has to take place in the stems. Many cacti have a second line of defence in the form of tufts of tiny barbed hairs, called glochidia (from the Greek word *glokhis*, meaning the barb of an arrow), which sit around the base of the spines. These barbs can work their way into the skin and are almost impossible to remove. For cacti enthusiasts, the resulting dermatitis is an occupational hazard, which left untreated can lead to acute inflammation for several months. In the wild, an animal attempting to eat the fleshy stem of a cactus is unlikely to forget the experience. Even if the wounds do not become infected and the animal survives the contact, it will not repeat the mistake.

Acacias are also known for their physical defences. Africa's wait-a-bit thorn is so named because the sharp, backward-pointing thorns on whip-like branches easily snag clothing and skin. Struggling when caught only

HARD TO GET The prickly pear cactus is edible, its juicy flesh tasting of green beans. Some birds manage to get past the sharp defensive barbs to reach the fruit – and so help to distribute the plant's seeds.

DO NOT TOUCH

**BRUSHING UP AGAINST A STINGING
NETTLE RESULTS IN A STING
FOLLOWED BY A RED, ITCHY RASH.**
It is an example of the chemical defence systems used by
some plants, as opposed to physical ones, such as thorns
or spines. These chemical defences are so efficient that just touching the
plants can be unpleasant, even dangerous.

The stinging nettle is a widespread weed throughout North America,
Europe and Asia, commonly found at woodland edges and on wasteland. The
entire plant is covered in poison-filled hairs, designed to trigger at the slightest
touch. The poisonous chemicals, including formic acid and histamine, are stored
in the bulbous base of each hair, while the tip of the hair is encrusted with
silicates, making it very brittle. The tip easily breaks when touched, turning into
a sharp lance that pierces the skin. The pressure that results from being
touched transfers from the needle tip to the bulbous poison reservoir, which
squirts out its contents. In this way the nettle delivers its irritant chemicals

ARMED ALL OVER A stinging nettle (Urtica dioica)
*carries its chemical deterrents in hollow hairs with
sharp, brittle tips. The hairs cover the stems as well
as the leaves of the plant and act like an array of
hypodermic needles if touched.*

right under the skin. With so many hairs primed and ready to inject their poison, the effect builds up.

Although the nettle's defences successfully deter animals such as rabbits, smaller creatures can crawl among the hairs unharmed and may even use them as protection. The tiny caterpillars of tortoiseshell, red admiral and peacock butterflies, as well as adult aphids, happily chomp their way through nettle leaves, managing to evade the stinging hairs as they go. Humans, too, have benefited from nettles. In medieval Europe, painful rheumatic joints were treated with 'urtication' (after the nettle's Latin name *Urtica*), which involved whipping them with nettles. In modern herbal medicine, nettle is still a useful treatment for rheumatism, although it is now taken rather less painfully as a tea that helps the body to eliminate sodium and urea.

Painful oil

Another well-known stinging plant is poison ivy, found throughout North America. Its weapon is urushiol oil, carried in its sap, which produces an allergic rash. The chemical is exuded at points where the plant has been damaged – or chewed, if any unfortunate creature has taken a bite. In theory, it is possible to touch poison ivy and remain unscathed so long as the foliage is intact, but it is best not to try, since the clear oily sap is difficult to see and can remain active, even on a dead plant, for up to five years.

Humans vary in their sensitivity to urushiol oil, but 90 per cent have some sort of reaction, and just a billionth of a gram can cause an itchy red rash that may last several weeks. The rash, which in severe cases can turn into fluid-filled blisters, usually appears a day or two after contact but can take up to a week. Someone coming into contact with poison ivy – either by direct touch or via clothing, boots, or garden equipment – has 15 minutes to react. Within 15 minutes, plain soap and water should get rid of the chemical, but once it has bonded with the proteins in the skin there is little that can be done to remove it.

THREE FOR DANGER Poison ivy may have reddish-orange leaves in autumn and can be confused with the benign Virginia creeper – although the latter generally has five leaflets, while poison ivy has three.

Poison ivy should never be burned: the smoke carries particles of sap, so inhaling it can result in an all-over rash and may be fatal.

Giant hogweed, native to the Caucasus Mountains of south-western Asia, looks like a huge cow parsley, with hollow, ribbed, purple-blotched stems that can be up to 5 m high. These bear deeply toothed leaves up to 1 m across and flat-topped clusters of white flowers. The Victorians brought giant hogweed to Britain for its ornamental value, and it soon escaped into the wild; it is now common along riverbanks and one of the most dangerous plants in the country. Like the stinging nettle, giant hogweed is covered in tiny hairs, which deliver its poisonous sap at the merest touch. The poison photosensitises the skin so that exposure to sunlight brings a severe and painful reaction. About 15–20 hours after contact with sap and sunlight, large, watery blisters appear. Healing is slow and painful, and scarring can be permanent.

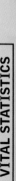

ONGAONGA

NEW ZEALAND'S NETTLE TREE HAS A STING

SO POISONOUS THAT IT CAN SERIOUSLY HARM AND EVEN KILL A PERSON.

Known to the Maoris as ongaonga, the nettle tree is a relative of the stinging nettle that grows up to 3 m tall. It is found all over New Zealand, preferring the edges of forests, where it forms dense impenetrable thickets. Ongaonga also often grows around cave entrances, which explains the name of New Zealand's deepest cavern – Nettlebed.

The stems of the nettle tree, its light green, jagged leaves and even its long flower spikes are all covered with large, white stinging hairs, primed to inject excruciating poison at the slightest touch. Besides a painful rash and sometimes numbness, the toxin provokes a histamine response that in severe cases can lead to breathing difficulties, convulsions and death. Although only a few human fatalities have been reported, several dogs and horses have died after blundering into a thicket and panicking amongst the stinging leaves.

VITAL STATISTICS

CLASS: Magnoliopsida
ORDER: Urticales
SPECIES: *Urtica ferox*
HABITAT: Coastal shrublands, woodland edges
DISTRIBUTION: New Zealand
KEY FEATURE: It is the deadliest stinging plant

PLANT POISONS

MANY PLANTS CARRY FOUL-TASTING, TOXIC SUBSTANCES IN THEIR TISSUES. Irises, lily of the valley, bleeding heart, ivy, holly, autumn crocus, daffodils and rhododendron all contain poisonous chemicals. Rhubarb leaves have tiny crystals of calcium oxalate, which cause burning and irritation to the mouth and tongue. Rather than delivering poison using stings, these plants rely on a bad taste and a range of other unpleasant, even lethal, effects to deter any animals inclined to eat them.

Nervous attack

The purple-hooded flowers of monkshood grow across Europe in shady hedgerows and along woodland edges. The plant looks attractive, but it contains in its sap one of the plant kingdom's strongest nerve poisons: aconitine. The poison is present throughout the plant and any contact with a living monkshood – even inhaling its scent – is dangerous. Symptoms of poisoning include a dry mouth, fever and delerium, ending in convulsions and sometimes death. For humans, just 10 g of the root delivers a fatal dose.

Some plant families specialise in poisons. The *Solanaceae*, which include the nightshades, henbane, horse nettle, thornapple, mandrake and tobacco, contain compounds called alkaloids, most of which are poisonous to some degree and some of which can be lethal. Among them is atropine, the main poison in deadly

LIQUID DEFENCES Chemicals in euphorbia sap cause painful inflammation of the nose, mouth and eyes. If ingested, it acts as a purgative – hence the plant's common name: spurge.

nightshade, which acts on the nervous system to slow the heart, obstruct breathing and cause hallucinations. In tobacco, the active ingredient is nicotine, which in the wild acts as a toxin against insect pests. Edible plants such as potatoes and tomatoes also belong to the *Solanaceae* family, but in their case the poisons are in the green parts of the plant.

The deadly poison cyanide is present in about a thousand plant species – for example, in the stones of apricots, peaches and plums. Some plants, such as certain species of hydrangea, have it in their leaves, where the cyanide is bound up with sugars in an inert form. Damaging the leaves – as when an insect bites into them – releases an enzyme that turns the compounds into poisonous cyanide gas. Although the fast-acting poison is enough to kill or deter most creatures, certain aphids and caterpillars can tolerate it, allowing them to feed with impunity while making them unpalatable to predators.

Perhaps the most notorious plant poison is ricin, derived from the waste mash of castor beans after they have been processed for their oil. Just 1 mg of ricin may be enough to kill an adult human. Ricin effectively paralyses human body cells by attacking the sites where proteins are made. Death is slow and painful – there may be excessive sweating, breathing difficulties and widespread organ failure. There is no known antidote. Treatment for suspected ricin poisoning centres on trying to rid the body of the toxin through blood transfusions.

10 DEADLY PLANTS

The world's most poisonous plants contain a variety of deadly toxins.

NAME (*SCIENTIFIC NAME*)	TOXIC PARTS	ACTIVE INGREDIENTS
Castor oil plant (*Ricinus communis*)	Seeds	Ricin
Deadly nightshade (*Atropa belladonna*)	All	Atropine, scopolamine, hyoscyamine
Foxglove (*Digitalis purpurea*)	All	Digitoxin, digitalin, digitalein, digitonin
Hemlock (*Conium maculatum*)	All	Coniine
Henbane (*Hyoscyamus niger*)	Seeds	Atropine, scopolamine, hyoscyamine
Ignatius' bean (*Strychnos ignatii*)	Seeds	Strychnine
Monkshood (*Aconitum napellus*)	All	Aconitine
Rosary pea (*Abrus precatorius*)	Seeds	Abrin
Thornapple (*Datura stramonium*)	All	Atropine, scopolamine, hyoscyamine
Yew (*Taxus baccata*, below)	All	Taxine

SURVIVING
ADVERSITY

THE EXPOSED SIDE OF A MOUNTAIN IS NOT THE EASIEST PLACE FOR A TREE TO GROW. As altitude increases, soils become poorer, there is less available water and the average temperature drops. Even conifers – the trees best adapted to such conditions – have a tough time here, in the face of constant harsh winds. But plants want to survive and when not protecting themselves from hungry herbivores, they are busy coping with the weather, showing a remarkable ability to adapt to less than perfect conditions.

On exposed mountainsides, the strength and persistence of the wind results in a growth form called 'flagging'. Although trees naturally grow straight up, ice-laden mountain winds strip foliage from their windward side, while the leaves and branches

SHAPED BY WIND Westerly gales blasting the slopes of the Pouakai Range on New Zealand's North Island have stripped and battered these mountain cedar trees so that they stoop away from the wind, leaving the windward side naked of foliage, in a growth pattern known as flagging. Protected by the cedars, shorter vegetation survives unscathed.

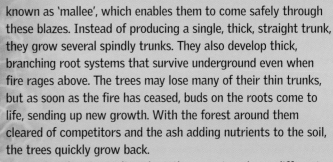

known as 'mallee', which enables them to come safely through these blazes. Instead of producing a single, thick, straight trunk, they grow several spindly trunks. They also develop thick, branching root systems that survive underground even when fire rages above. The trees may lose many of their thin trunks, but as soon as the fire has ceased, buds on the roots come to life, sending up new growth. With the forest around them cleared of competitors and the ash adding nutrients to the soil, the trees quickly grow back.

Another Australian plant, the grass tree, has a different strategy for surviving wild fire. Its 'trunk' is composed not of wood but of an inner fibrous stem surrounded by tightly compacted leaf bases, sealed with a yellowish fire-retardant gum. During a blaze, the topknot of long leaves ignites like a torch, but the tough, closely packed foliage around the stem protects the growing point within. A few months later, the plant sends out a long, thin spike covered in thousands of tiny white flowers, ready to be pollinated and to set seeds.

GRASS GLUE Australia's Aboriginal people used the yellow fireproof sap of grass trees as a glue to attach spear heads to their shafts. Grass trees are very slow-growing – a 2 m tall specimen could be 200 years old.

on the downwind side survive and grow. Bending away from the prevailing wind to lessen wind resistance, the trees end up looking like flags. Another way in which trees everywhere adapt to prevailing winds is by building up stronger tissue on the windward side. If the wind constantly blows from the east, a tree will lay down thick-walled strengthening cells on that side.

A tree's resistance to a sudden burst of wind – as during a storm or hurricane – depends on its root structure. Trees with deep taproots generally fare better than trees with shallow root networks. Conifers are adapted to take the fiercest winds, with deep taproots and tiny needles that give little wind resistance. Broad-leaved trees vary in how they cope with high winds. They drop their leaves in the autumn in readiness for the worst winter weather, but disaster can strike when high winds come earlier than usual. The effects of Britain's October 1987 storm were made worse because the trees were still in leaf.

Out of the fire

In parched climates, wild fires are a regular occurrence as lightning ignites tinder-dry landscapes. In south-western Australia, the eucalyptus trees grow in a distinctive form

END OF THE LINE

OF ALL THE THREATS THAT PLANTS FACE, THE DEADLIEST COME FROM MINUTE ORGANISMS, often invisible to the naked eye – fungi, bacteria and viruses. More than 8000 fungi cause plant diseases, including mildew, grey mould, rusts, smuts, ringspot and wilt. Bacterial diseases include rots, cankers and blights. The most common symptoms of viral infections are stunted growth and a 'mosaic' patterning of light and dark patches in a plant's leaves.

Elm disaster

One of the most catastrophic diseases of recent times was the fungal Dutch elm disease, which killed 30 million elms in Britain in the 1970s. Fungi reproduce by spores, which travel from plant to plant on the wind, in splashes of rainwater or carried by an animal, called a vector. The fungus–vector partnership is especially lethal, because the animal takes the disease right to its target.

The vector for Dutch elm disease is the elm bark beetle. The cycle begins when a female beetle seeks out a tree in which to lay her eggs. She prefers a diseased tree because there may be cracks in the bark allowing her to get between the bark and the wood. The eggs hatch and the grubs chew galleries through the bark, eventually becoming adult beetles. Because the tree is diseased, it is riddled with long thread-like fungus strands (hyphae), which

deposit sticky spores along the beetle tunnels. When the young beetles emerge, they fly to a healthy tree, carrying the spores with them. In the new tree, the fungus starts to infiltrate the water-conducting vessels (xylem, see page 22). The tree reacts by plugging up the xylem with gums and resins in a vain effort to isolate the infection. The combination of gums and fungal growth blocks the xylem so that the tree dies of thirst.

Bacterial diseases, such as canker, usually occur in plants stressed by another disease. Bacteria get inside the weakened plant – transmitted by rain splashes or animal vectors – and start to reproduce rapidly, destroying tissue and releasing toxins. Viruses infect plants by moving from cell to cell, replicating themselves as they go – a plant infected with mosaic virus may have as many as 10 million virus particles in one cell. Sap-sucking insects, such as aphids, often transmit the viruses, picking up the particles as they feed on diseased plants. The virus stays alive in the insect's gut, and when the insect moves on to a new plant, the virus travels down its mouthparts into the sap of the new host.

A LOSING BATTLE The trunk of an apricot tree infected with bacterial canker oozes thick amber-coloured gum as the tree tries to stop the bacteria spreading through its tissues.

CHAIN OF DEATH An elm bark beetle and its larvae (above) burrow into elm bark. The elm's tendency to shoot from the roots to form a line of trees (left) makes it vulnerable to disease. If one tree becomes infected, the disease quickly spreads to the others in the line.

GREEN
WEALTH

GRAPEVINES IN THE ALSACE REGION OF FRANCE STRETCH OUT IN ORDERLY ROWS. In France alone there are around 800 000 hectares of vineyards yielding some 7 to 8 billion bottles of wine each year. Mankind has harnessed the plant world into an abundance of commodities. Its bounty includes staple crops, such as rice, wheat and potatoes, a cornucopia of herbs and spices, and a sensual feast of flowers. We derive sugar from the sap of plants and oils from their seeds. They provide refreshment in the form of tea, coffee and cocoa. We clothe ourselves in textiles made from plant fibres, such as cotton and linen, while timber, furniture and paper are just some of the many products derived from trees. Plants also have the power to heal, forming the basis of many modern pharmaceutical drugs as well as traditional herbal remedies.

GLOBAL
HARVEST

MAIZE, RICE AND WHEAT WERE AMONG THE EARLIEST GRASSES TO BE CULTIVATED BY MAN. They remain the world's staple crops today, providing half of all plant-derived food energy. Other important crops include rye, oats and barley in temperate regions, and sorghum and millet in the tropics. Crops that are not grasses but produce a high-protein, cereal-like grain include quinoa from Peru and buckwheat from north-eastern Asia.

LABOUR INTENSIVE In 2007, more than 418 million tonnes of rice were grown around the world, 127 million of them in China. Other important growers include India, Indonesia, Bangladesh and Vietnam. Paddy fields, like this one in Bali, remain largely unmechanised.

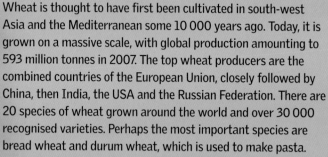

Wheat is thought to have first been cultivated in south-west Asia and the Mediterranean some 10 000 years ago. Today, it is grown on a massive scale, with global production amounting to 593 million tonnes in 2007. The top wheat producers are the combined countries of the European Union, closely followed by China, then India, the USA and the Russian Federation. There are 20 species of wheat grown around the world and over 30 000 recognised varieties. Perhaps the most important species are bread wheat and durum wheat, which is used to make pasta.

Rice was first domesticated in Asia at least 5000 years ago, and this region remains by far the largest producer and consumer. Modern varieties of rice have been developed that grow rapidly in warm, tropical conditions, producing three crops a year.

Maize originated in the Mexican highlands, where its wild ancestor was first farmed some 6000 years ago. Today, there are thousands of varieties, adapted to so many different climates that maize is grown all over the world. The USA was the single largest producer of maize in 2007, growing some 267 million tonnes (out of a global total of 704 million). It was followed by China, the European Union, Brazil and Argentina.

Providing for the future

The need to feed an ever-increasing global population requires greater and greater yields, and crops that are more tolerant to drought and other adverse environmental conditions. One avenue being explored by agriculturists is genetic engineering. This relatively new technology allows the characteristics of crops to be changed far more quickly than a standard breeding programme. Scientists take genes with desirable characteristics from the cells of one plant and transfer them directly into the cells of another. Using this technique it is possible to transfer genes from a totally unrelated plant or even a different organism.

For example, adding certain genes from the bacterium *Bacillus thuringiensis* to maize results in plants that produce the Bt toxin, which is lethal to a number of insect pests.

Although there are many genetically modified (GM) crops now being grown around the world, with the largest producer being the USA, the technology divides opinion. Environmentalists point to the lessons that were painfully learned after the widespread use of agrochemicals in the 1960s, such as DDT, which turned out to have dire consequences for both the environment and human health. They argue that GM crops may have adverse side effects on local ecosystems, and that they may affect human health, causing allergies and perhaps other unforseen problems.

VITAL HARVEST A combine harvester works its way through a wheat field in Wiltshire, England. It has been estimated that wheat accounts for up to 20 per cent of daily calorific intake in the West.

CORNUCOPIA

IT HAS BEEN ESTIMATED THAT OF THE 300 000 PLANTS KNOWN, around 30 000 species are edible. Yet only about 200 have been widely domesticated. From those naturally occurring species, thousands of varieties (or cultivars) have been developed. Since the plants were first cultivated, farmers all over the world have repeatedly selected and bred plants with desirable characteristics, leading to the great diversity and more productive varieties now available.

The cabbage is one of the world's most widely cultivated vegetables. It belongs to a group of plants called brassicas (or crucifers), which also includes cauliflowers, kale, Brussels sprouts, Chinese leaf, pak choi (Chinese cabbage), turnip, broccoli and mustard. Wild cabbage originated in southern Europe, though today it is grown as far afield as the USA, Russia, Japan, and China, which is by far the world's largest producer. The green

BOATLOADS OF GOODNESS Much of the produce on display in Bangkok's floating market will be unfamiliar to most Westerners. Only a fraction of the exotic fruit and vegetables grown there ever reaches Europe.

leafy brassicas are particularly rich in vitamins C and K. They are also a good source of vitamin E, potassium, folate and thiamine. In traditional medicine raw cabbage juice may be prescribed to treat a gastric ulcer, while a compress of cabbage leaves is used to treat leg ulcers, eczema and shingles.

A taste for the exotic

The banana, which grows naturally in the tropics and subtropics, is the world's most-eaten fruit. Key to the banana's success is that it can be picked when unripe and allowed to ripen en route to

CABBAGE HARVEST Cruciferous vegetables, which include cabbages, are one of the main food crops worldwide. All crucifers contain compounds called indoles and other nutrients that may offer some protection against cancer.

market. A native to Indonesia and Malaysia, the banana plant is now cultivated all over the tropics. Brazil, India and Thailand produce large crops, mostly for domestic consumption. The largest exporters include Ecuador, Costa Rica and Colombia.

There are dozens of different varieties of cultivated banana, mostly derived from two wild species: *Musa acuminata* and *M. balbisiana*. Unusually, the fruits of the banana plant develop from female flowers without the need for them to be pollinated, which is why most cultivated bananas have no seeds. The flowers, and consequently fruit, are held in long flower heads, so that each complete bunch holds about 200 'fingers', as the individual fruits are known, and weighs about 40 kg.

All bananas are a good source of carbohydrate and potassium. The dessert varieties can be left to ripen and consumed raw. Common varieties include the large yellow 'Cavendish' and 'Williams', but there are many others. Red bananas have a reddish skin and pinkish flesh; apple bananas from Brazil are small, greenish and taste a bit like apples; 'Lady's Finger' is a very small and especially sweet variety from Thailand. Cooking bananas, including plantains, are used while they are still

unripe (green). They are drier and contain more starch than dessert varieties so need to be cooked. Plantains are often used to make banana chips. The fibres of another type of banana (*M. textilis*) are used to make ropes and paper.

Bananas can be grown outside the tropics if they are kept warm under glass. They are famously cultivated in Iceland in greenhouses heated by the country's abundant natural geothermal resources, profiting from the long hours of summer daylight.

Along with the universally popular banana, supermarkets are stocking an ever-growing selection of other exotic fruits. There is the pale-green, scaly skinned custard apple from Peru, the waxy, yellow star fruit from Sri Lanka and the aptly named ugli fruit from Jamaica, which looks like a saggy grapefruit but tastes more like a tangerine. For chocoholics there is the black sapote from Mexico, whose pulp has the flavour and consistency of chocolate pudding.

Perhaps the most challenging of all for Western palates is the durian fruit from South-east Asia, which locals call the 'King of fruits'. The silky, yellow flesh tastes something like crème brûlée and almonds, but the thorny fruit, larger than a mango, exudes an unpleasant, pervasive odour that has been variously described as rotten onions, armpits, pig manure and sewers. In Singapore the fruit is banned on public transport due to its pervasive odour. Anyone who consumes the delicacy will also have unsavoury 'durian breath' for several hours afterwards.

BURIED TREASURE

AFTER CEREALS, THE WORLD'S MOST IMPORTANT CROP IS THE POTATO. Originally from South America, potatoes were brought back to Europe in the late-16th century and are now grown all over the world, from southern Greenland to New Zealand. Potatoes are cultivated mainly for their carbohydrate content, though they contain other nutrients, particularly vitamin C. They belong to the same family of plants as deadly nightshade, and as such they contain the poisonous chemical solanine in their leaves and stems.

In Europe all the cultivars that are grown today have been bred from one species: *Solanum tuberosum*. Potatoes became a staple in northern Europe and Russia, because they would grow in the harshest of climates, when other crops failed. Varieties have been bred specifically for use in monocultures, to produce crops with high yields and resistance to disease.

Potatoes are still grown some 4200 m up in the Andes, where most other types of crop would falter. Andean farmers maintain a broad base of varieties, with hundreds of wild species and thousands of cultivated forms to choose from. The tubers vary in shape, size and colour and are given their own names, such as 'potato that makes young brides weep' for a particularly knobbly type that is difficult to peel. Typically, an Andean farmer plants 20 different varieties in one field, a practice that has kept alive a diverse and valuable range.

There are other tuber crops grown widely in the Andes that are virtually unknown beyond South America. Ullucu or papa lisa (*Ullucus tuberosus*) produces smooth bulbous tubers, about 20 cm across, that may be yellow, pink, purple or red, while the brilliantly coloured, long, rough tubers of oca (*Oxalis tuberosus*) can be very sweet. Mashua or ainu (*Tropaeolum tuberosum*) produces long, rough tubers that are very resistant to cold. All three plants are important food crops in Columbia, Peru, Ecuador and Bolivia. The crops are hardly touched by pests and diseases and could potentially be grown as extensively as the potato.

Tubers in the tropics

Though potatoes do well in northern climes and at high altitudes, they are not a reliable crop in the tropics. Other root and tuber crops – including yams, cassava and sweet potato – are much

ESSENTIAL CARBS Cassava (above) and sweet potatoes (left) store starches in their tuberous roots, making them an excellent source of carbohydrates.

better suited to a hot, wet climate. Cassava (or manioc) comes from the large tubers of *Manihot esculenta*, which belongs to the same family as the rubber tree. The plant originated in tropical America and was introduced to West Africa in the 16th century. Today, it is a staple food in Africa and South America, where around 500 million people eat it daily. There are two types: a relatively sweet-tasting cultivar and a bitter-tasting one. Both carry toxins that must be removed before the carbohydrate-rich flesh can be consumed. The sweet cultivar has the toxin in its skin, so only needs to be peeled before cooking, while the bitter type has the toxin throughout its flesh and requires more time-consuming preparation. First the flesh is grated and pounded; then it is washed and drained several times and left to stand overnight.

The flesh can then be used to make flat breads, or dried and powdered, while the extracted juice is fermented into a strong liquor called Kasiri.

Another important tuber, the yam, comes from the root of a group of vines that grow in tropical America, Asia and Africa. The vines belong to the genus *Dioscorea* – different species and their cultivars are grown in different countries. White guinea yam (*Dioscorea rotundata*) is the most important species in Africa, while water yam (*D. alata*) and lesser yam (*D. esculenta*) are grown in Asia. Yam tubers are smooth and cylindrical with a white flesh and can grow to enormous sizes, with the biggest over 2 m long and weighing up to 70 kg. Yams are key to survival in West Africa and New Guinea. Higher levels of protein in the yam tubers make them more nutritious than other major root crops. Another important factor is that the tubers can be stored for months even in the tropical climate.

Like cassava, yams usually have a poisonous skin, which must be removed before eating. They can then be used in much the same way as potatoes – boiled, fried, baked or roasted – but are somewhat sweeter. In Africa yams are usually boiled, peeled and pounded to a pulp in a traditional wooden pestle and mortar to make a thick dough known as 'fufu'.

Certain species of yam, particularly Mexican yam, contain diosgenin, a chemical that can be converted into the female hormones progesterone and oestrogen. When the American chemist Russell Marker discovered this fact in 1942, Mexican yams became the basis of the oral-contraceptive industry. In the West the contraceptive pill is now made from synthetic versions of the chemicals, but yams are still grown in China for their diosgenin content.

Sweet potatoes are not related to potatoes, but are the tubers of a trailing vine called *Ipomoea batatas*. The tubers are smooth and tapered with a flesh that is usually orange, but may be yellow or purple. The plants are native to both sides of the Pacific, occurring in tropical regions of America as well as Polynesia, and were brought back to Europe by Christopher Columbus in the late-15th century. The tubers have long been a popular food in the southern states of the USA, where they are often erroneously referred to as yams. As well as providing starch and fibre, sweet potatoes are a good source of betacarotene. Today, they are grown widely throughout the tropics and subtropics, the largest producer being China.

While grains and tubers are the major staple foods around the world, there are other parts of plants that can be harvested for their carbohydrates. Taro, for example, is the swollen, starchy corms (thickened underground stem bases) of *Colocasia esculenta,* a plant belonging to the arum family, while sago is a starch made from the pith inside the trunks of the sago palm (*Metroxylon sagu*).

YAM FESTIVAL In Papua New Guinea, yams are the only form of carbohydrate that can be easily stored. The harvest in May and June is a time for celebration, when the year's crop is piled high.

DAILY REFRESHMENT

OVER HALF OF THE WORLD'S POPULATION DRINK TEA, with the biggest consumers of all, the British, getting through 165 million cups of the refreshing infusion every day. Tea comes from the leaves of a small evergreen shrub, *Camellia sinensis* – a plant native to mainland south and South-east Asia, but today cultivated in many parts of the world. Legend has it that the Chinese emperor Shen Nung discovered tea more than 4000 years ago, when a few leaves fell from a tea bush into some boiling hot water. Today, there are over 1500 varieties, with many subtleties of flavour. Teas from China, the world's largest producer followed by India, include lapsang souchong, gunpowder, keemun and oolong. Indian teas include assam, a dark, malty tea, and darjeeling, which is grown only on 100 estates in the foothills of the Himalayas and is considered the 'champagne of teas'. The most widely consumed teas are blends of several types and qualities.

Black tea, which is made by rolling, fermenting and drying the leaves, constitutes most of the tea drunk in Europe and North America, while green tea, which is unfermented, is more popular in the East. The freshly picked leaves are simply steamed and dried, producing a more delicate flavour. A third type is 'white' tea, which is produced from the freshly picked buds of the tea bushes.

A cup of coffee

Another universally popular beverage, coffee is thought to have originated in Ethiopia in the 2nd century AD, where berries of the native plant *Coffea arabica* were fermented into a stimulating

TAKING TEA Every 7 to 10 days a new flush of tip growth is ready to be harvested from tea bushes. Plantation workers, like these in Sri Lanka, do this by hand, some gathering 30 kg of leaves and buds a day.

drink (thanks to the beans' high caffeine content). By the early 18th century coffee had reached Europe and coffeehouses began to spring up selling this fashionable new drink. Today, coffee is an important cash crop grown in some 80 tropical and subtropical countries. *C. arabica* remains the dominant species, accounting for 70 per cent of the market, with Brazil its biggest producer by far. Another species, *C. canephora*, produces 'robusta' coffee, which is grown principally in Vietnam, the world's second biggest coffee producer. Although inferior in flavour to arabica, robusta is easier to grow in less-favourable climates. It also has a higher caffeine content and is often used in instant-coffee blends.

The most expensive coffee in the world, known as kopi luwak, is produced from beans that have travelled through the digestive system of the rare Indonesian palm civet. Gourmets say that the special flavour is due to the animal's habit of choosing only the ripest, most flavoursome beans from bushes growing in the Sumatran forest. The beans are cleaned thoroughly before being roasted and served up at £380 per kg.

BERRIES TO BEANS Coffee berries take eight months to ripen on the bush, each berry yielding two coffee beans.

Divine drink

Though wild cocoa trees are native to the rain forests of South America, the use and cultivation of the beans began with the Maya and Aztecs of Central America. Both civilisations revered the tree and incorporated a drink made from its beans into their spiritual rituals. The cocoa tree is an understorey plant and traditionally plantations would recreate its preferred growing conditions by planting it under shade trees. But there are many cultivated forms and some can be grown in direct sunlight. The two most important types grown today are criollo and forastero. Criollo was the type grown by the Aztecs and produces the best-quality beans, while forastero is a hardier and higher yielding tree and is the type grown in West Africa, where most cocoa beans come from today.

RIPE PODS Cocoa pods develop from flowers on the main trunk of the tree. Each pod contains 20 to 60 beans held in a sticky white pulp. After harvesting, the cocoa beans and pulp are scooped from the pods and left to ferment before being dried.

SPICES AND HERBS

TODAY, PEPPER ACCOUNTS FOR ONE-FIFTH OF THE WORLD'S SPICE TRADE. It is a store-cupboard staple in most homes, but centuries ago adding it to food was a bit like sprinkling on gold-dust. Peppercorns, which grow on a vine that is native to the south-west coast of India, were once so rare and valuable that they were used as a form of collateral or currency. In his *Natural History*, written in the first century AD, Pliny the Elder bemoaned that 'there is no year in which India does not drain the Roman Empire of fifty million sesterces.' And it is said that when Attila the Hun sacked Rome in the 5th century AD, he demanded a ton of pepper from the Romans as a ransom.

Like the cinnamon that grew in Ceylon, the star anise from China and the nutmeg, cloves and other exotic spices from the Spice Islands in Indonesia (now known as the Molucca Islands), the only way for the pepper to reach Europe was via the ancient trade routes that connected with the East. The Spice Route developed over thousands of years, stretching from the west coast of Japan, through the Indonesian islands to China and around the coast of India. Spices travelled overland by caravan or were shipped from India to the Middle East and then across the Mediterranean to Europe. For centuries the countries of Arabia controlled the supply and were able to set their own prices. They tried to keep their sources secret and encouraged wild and strange stories about how the spices were harvested. With such mysterious origins, spices were imbued with magical powers.

At the end of the 13th century a young Venetian adventurer, Marco Polo, returned from an epic journey to the East. He told first-hand accounts of the countries where spices were grown; he had visited India and seen its great ports and spice markets. At last the secret of the source was out – and it was not so mysterious after all. With the price of spices reaching extortionate levels and the demand showing no signs of diminishing, the nations of Europe set out to find their own supplies. Adventurers from Portugal set sail to find a new sea route to the East. The first to find a direct route by sea to the fabled land of spices was Portuguese adventurer, Vasco da Gama, who sailed around the Cape of Good Hope to Mozambique and then to India. A few years earlier Spain had sent Christopher Columbus to find a western route to India and he ended up discovering America in 1492. Soon the Dutch and English joined in and during the 16th century there was a free-for-all as the various countries scrambled to secure a piece of this lucrative market. The competition could be fierce, sparking wars and skirmishes over four centuries.

PEPPER PLANT *Black pepper is made from the dried unripe berries (peppercorns) of* Piper nigrum. *The hotness derives from a constituent called piperine. White pepper is derived from the seed of fully ripe berries.*

INDIAN SPICE *Aromatic spices on sale in a market in Goa on the west coast of India. The Portuguese seized Goa in 1510 in order to control the lucrative spice trade.*

Though driven by the aim of finding their fortunes, they became the discoverers of new continents.

When Columbus stumbled upon America, he was, in fact, looking for India and its famous spice of pepper. Instead, he found a group of islands, which he called the West Indies. He also found chillies and because of their characteristic hot, pungent taste, he called them peppers. The confusion remains to this day, despite the fact that chillies and pepper belong to entirely different plant families and originate on different continents.

DOUBLE SPICE *The lacy reddish covering on a nutmeg seed is there to attract the birds, but it can be removed and dried to produce mace. By the 17th century the Dutch controlled the trade in nutmeg, sometimes destroying the seeds to prevent them being propagated by their competitors.*

GINGER PLANT Ginger is the hot-tasting underground root-like stem of the ginger plant (Zingiber officianale). The medicinal benefits of ginger, which include alleviating the symptoms of nausea and influenza, have been known to Chinese herbalists for thousands of years.

flower of a crocus (see page 135), and vanilla, which comes from an orchid pod, both of which must be harvested by hand.

Healthy herbs

Like spices, herbs have long been prized for therapeutic and culinary properties. Lavender, rosemary, basil, mint, thyme, oregano, lemon grass, tarragon, parsley – these are just some of

Spices are the dried fruit, bark, seed or root of a plant and have a wide range of culinary and medicinal uses. Cinnamon comes from the bark of evergreen trees growing in Sri Lanka and China. Older bark is used to make ground cinnamon, while young bark is peeled from outer branches to make cinnamon sticks. Cloves are dried flower buds, while ginger and turmeric come from rhizomes (modified root-like stems). Tamarind is the pulp from seedpods, while cumin, fennel and dried coriander are seeds. Two of today's most expensive spices are saffron, derived from the

PUNGENT LEAVES Chives are the smallest species of the onion family. They are grown for their long, hollow, grass-like leaves, which are chopped into a variety of dishes to impart a subtle onion flavour.

the many herbs whose very names conjure up a particular flavour, aroma or association with a region or country.

Practically every culture has built up its own extensive knowledge of herbs and their benefical properties. The prehistoric cave drawings at Lascaux in France feature herbs, while archaeological evidence shows that ancient Egyptian priests regularly used herbal medicine, with a repertory of hundreds of medicinal plants, some of which are still in use today. In the 5th century BC, the Greek physician Hippocrates listed hundreds of useful herbs, including anise to treat coughs. In the 1st century AD, the Greek physician Dioscorides wrote *De Materia Medica*, a compendium of over 500 plants and their medicinal properties. In India the tradition of herbal medicine goes back over 5000 years. It forms part of a holistic system called Ayurvedic medicine that is still in use today. Ayurvedic principles relate to three fundamental energy types, or 'doshas', called vata, pitta and kapha. Every person has their own prevailing dosha and the Ayurvedic practitioner prescribes herbal remedies accordingly, choosing from over 1000 types of plant. Patients are normally prescribed their own appropriate mixture. For example, someone with a kapha temperament (tends to be overweight and lethargic) may be given invigorating herbs, such as ginger or chilli.

China has its own system of herbal medicine with its roots in antiquity. It is influenced by Taoist philosophy and the central concept of balance between yin and yang to encourage the flow of chi, or qi – universal energy – through the body. Interruption of the flow can lead to illness and disease, so Chinese herbal medicine aims to restore balance to the body. Herbal medicines go hand in hand with acupuncture, used to release blockages in the energy flow. The system also incorporates the theory of the five elements: earth, metal, water, wood and fire, which are associated with certain emotions, organs and plants. In Chinese medicine, ginger is considered a yang plant and would be prescribed for a yin

RED HOT Chillies were discovered by Christopher Columbus in America and taken by European sailors to India and the East, where they were soon incorporated into regional dishes. The fiery heat associated with chilli peppers is produced by chemicals known as capsaicinoids.

herbalism began to record the information and try to order it into a coherent science, yet still much of it remained imbued with superstition. Early herbalism was based on the 'doctrine of signatures', whereby a plant would indicate the disease it was best suited to cure from the shape and structure of its parts. In 1652 the English herbalist and astrologer Nicholas Culpeper wrote *The English Physitian* in reaction to the new practice of scientific medicine that was emerging at the time. Culpeper's book, which included a list of herbs appropriated to a particular planet, did much to bring herbalism to the general public and continued to be popular until superseded by chemists and mainstream medical practice from the 19th century onwards. Nevertheless, herbalism experienced a resurgence in the 20th century, and many clinical studies have been carried out to try to determine how herbal medicines work.

Many of the attributes of herbs have now been verified by modern science. By isolating the herbs' constituents, chemists have tested them in the laboratory and found many of the traditional claims and recommended uses to be absolutely correct. A curious fact is that often a herb in its entirety is more effective than its isolated active constituents, even when they are administered together.

Herbalists use herbs in a number of ways. Some plants, such as garlic and ginger, can be used fresh and added to meals, while some are dried and used to make teas. These are usually the flowers, berries or leafy parts of the plant. The resulting teas, or infusions, may be consumed or used as a gargle. Sometimes the dried parts, including bark or roots, may be boiled in water for several minutes to make a decoction, which can be used in the same way as an infusion. Herbs can also be used externally as poultices and applied to the skin to soothe rashes or to ease aching limbs.

condition. Prescriptions usually contain several herbs in precise ratios and combinations based on an overall or holistic diagnosis of the patient's health. The Chinese herbalist has some 10 000 plant species to call upon, though in modern practice 500 species are commonly used.

In Britain the practice of herbal medicine is also ancient. It is thought to predate the Druids, and has been handed down through word of mouth. Remnants of the earliest uses of herbs can be seen in the common names of wild plants. For example, eyebright is used in a compress to treat eye conditions, such as conjunctivitis, while feverfew has long been used to ease a fever. Heartsease is used to help heart conditions. The Druids had seven sacred herbs: clover, henbane, mistletoe, monkshood, pasqueflower, primrose and vervain. The herbs were more than medicinal, they were believed to have magical powers. Several early books on

HEALING HERBS

Some popular culinary herbs and their traditional medicinal uses.

HERB	TRADITIONAL USE
Basil	Aids digestion and eases stomach cramps
Camomile	Relieves anxiety and insomnia
Coriander	Tonic for the stomach and the heart
Dill	Relieves wind
Fennel	Aids digestion; relieves nausea
Mint	Aids digestion
Parsley	Freshens the breath
Rosemary	Stimulates nervous and circulatory systems
Sage	Eases indigestion; soothes sore throats
Thyme	Antiseptic, antibiotic and antifungal properties

SAFFRON

ONCE WORTH ITS WEIGHT IN GOLD, SAFFRON

REMAINS THE WORLD'S MOST EXPENSIVE SPICE. Named after the Arabic word *zafaran*, meaning yellow, it is harvested from the long red stigmas of a particular type of crocus. Selective breeding over the centuries has led to the development of a flower with particularly long stigmas, which protrude from the mauve-coloured petals. Each flower produces three stigmas and it takes around 75 000 flowers, harvested by hand, to yield just 500 g of dried saffron. Today good-quality saffron costs more than £2 for each gram.

Saffron was first cultivated over 4000 years ago and has long been used as an aromatic flavouring, perfume, dye and medicine. The ancient Greeks, Egyptians and Romans valued the spice as an aphrodisiac and sedative. Today, scientists are researching the potential of saffron as a treatment for cancer. Extracts of saffron have been shown to inhibit the growth of tumour cells and suppress the development of colon cancer. The cancer-fighting properties of saffron are attributed to one of its major components: a carotenoid called crocin.

The saffron crocus that we know today cannot produce seed and is unknown in the wild. Most is cultivated – by division of its rootstock – in Iran, which produces around 300 tonnes each year.

VITAL STATISTICS

CLASS: Liliopsida
ORDER: Asparagales
SPECIES: *Crocus sativus*
HABITAT: Mediterranean-type dry shrubland
DISTRIBUTION: Spain through the Mediterranean to India
KEY FEATURE: World's most expensive spice

PLANT MATERIALS

PEOPLE LEARNED HOW TO EXTRACT AND WEAVE PLANT FIBRES INTO FABRIC THOUSANDS OF YEARS AGO. Despite the relatively recent invention of synthetic, often cheaper, alternatives, plant fibres are still widely used today. Some remain very localised in their use, while others have become worldwide commodities, used to make all sorts of textiles.

Cotton is by far the most important plant fibre, used in 40 per cent of textiles worldwide. The fibre comes from the cotton plant's seedpod, or boll, which when ripe seems to explode into a mass of white fluffy fibres. The silky fibres are actually seed hairs that help the seeds to disperse in the wind and it is the structure of these tiny fibres that give cotton its many advantages as a textile. Each hair is hollow, which means that cotton is an absorbent fabric that 'breathes'. Kinks in the hairs enable them to lock together when twisted, making them naturally suited to being spun into thread. Cotton can be woven into varied fabrics, from strong heavy canvas to flimsy muslin and gauze. Egyptian cotton, which has especially fine, long fibres, is one of the most luxurious cottons. Today's leading cotton growers are China and America, while the major textile producers are India and Pakistan.

One of the oldest known textiles is a type of linen produced from the stems of flax, a wiry-stemmed herbaceous plant with striking blue flowers thought to have originated in the Middle East some 10 000 years ago and brought to Europe about 6000 years ago. The ancient Egyptians wrapped strips of the linen around their mummies. Today, the major flax-producing countries are Canada, the USA and China. The large seeds of some varieties of flax can be used to make linseed oil.

In Tonga and Fiji, ceremonial garments are still produced from pulped and beaten tree bark, while in the Philippines a particularly fine, gossamer-like fabric is made with fibres from a variety of pineapple with 2 m long leaves.

Cork and rubber

Cork comes from the bark of an evergreen type of oak tree from southern Europe. Combining lightness, durability and near-impermeability, cork is used for flooring, bottle stops, fishing floats and buoys. Cork has also been used in rocket technology due to its fire resistance. About 50 per cent of the world's cork is harvested in Portugal.

Another versatile material – rubber – comes from the rubber tree (*Hevea brasiliensis*), native to the Amazon rain forest, though it is now grown in plantations in Malaysia, Thailand and Indonesia. The rubber is contained in a milky latex situated between the cambium layer and the bark, which oozes out when the bark is cut. Raw latex is mixed with various compounds to make a durable rubber that does not crack or perish. Rubber – both natural and in its synthetic form, which is derived from petroleum – is used in many household and industrial products, including tyres, hosing, floor tiles, gloves and rubber bands.

ON TAP The milky latex of a rubber tree is extracted in a delicate process known as tapping. This involves cutting a groove that spirals round the trunk. Every other day a tiny piece of bark is taken from the lower edge, so that the groove can be tapped repeatedly. Each tapping collects about 50 g of latex.

KING COTTON Cotton fibres are actually seed hairs and each ripe boll contains two types. The longer lint hairs are around 2.5 cm long and used for textiles, while the 1 mm linter hairs are used to make felt, cotton wool, paper and other cellulose-based materials. It is thought that 1 kg of cotton contains around 200 million individual seed hairs.

SPANISH OLIVES Spain has over 2 million hectares of olive groves and is the world's largest producer of olives. Most are grown in Andalucia in the south.

and the International Olive Council has set up a strict set of rules governing how farmers may label their oil based on the way it has been processed. Top of the scale is first pressing 'extra virgin' oil, which means the oil has been extracted without chemicals and has less than 0.8 per cent acidity. It is superior to 'virgin' oil, which is produced the same way but has an acidity of up to 2 per cent, followed by 'ordinary olive oil' with acidity of up to 3.3 per cent. Next in quality (and price) is 'olive oil', which may be a blend of oils and include refined oil that has been obtained with chemicals.

ENERGY STORES

PLANTS SUCH AS SUNFLOWERS, CORN, COCONUT, PALM, SOYA, FLAX AND OILSEED RAPE have oil-rich seeds that yield oils used in a wide variety of products from cooking fat and margarines to soaps and lubricants. Olive oil has been harvested from the fruit of the olive, the quintessentially Mediterranean tree, for thousands of years and today there are around 750 million trees cultivated worldwide. The oil is a good source of vitamin E and contains vitamins A, D and K. It also contains between 60 and 80 per cent of monounsaturated fats (in this case, oleic acid), thought to reduce 'bad cholesterol' (LDL) and preserve 'good cholesterol' (HDL).

Olive trees grow slowly in the hot, dry climate and do not bear fruit until they are 5–10 years old. They reach their prime at the age of 35, but will go on producing a good crop until they are around 100 years old, after which the yield declines. The key to the perfect olive oil is judging the moment when the crop is ripe. Unripe olives produce a bitter oil, while overripe olives result in a rancid oil. Once picked the olives are crushed and then pressed to release the oils, with around 5 kg of olives making 1 litre of olive oil. Like fine wine, the oil is graded

OIL FIELDS Fields of dazzling yellow oilseed rape are a familiar sight throughout Europe, where most of it is grown. Rape was traditionally used as a fodder crop, but it is now widely grown for its oil.

Natural sweetness

Around 70 per cent of the world's sugar comes from sugar cane, with the remaining 30 per cent from sugar beet. While sugar cane grows only in the tropics, sugar beet can be grown in temperate climates, with France the largest producer. After harvesting, the leafy parts of the beet are used as fodder, while the thick, bulbous roots where the sugar is stored are boiled to produce a thick syrup, which crystallises into granules.

The sap of the maple, a tree that grows widely through North America, is another natural source of sugar. The tree is tapped in much the same way as rubber when the sap begins to rise in early spring. During the height of the 'sugaring season', which lasts six weeks, the sap contains between 2 and 5 per cent sugar. After collection the sap is boiled to concentrate its sugar, so it forms a syrup. Canada, and in particular Quebec, produces around 80 per cent of the world's maple syrup.

ALL PLANTS MAKE SUGARS, SUCH AS SUCROSE
AND FRUCTOSE, DURING PHOTOSYNTHESIS, BUT NONE MORE SO THAN SUGAR CANE.

This tropical grass, one of the tallest after bamboo, stores sucrose in its thick, jointed stem. Native to New Guinea and South-east Asia, it was one of the first crops to be taken to the Americas by early European settlers and it is now grown in plantations around the world. Brazil is the largest producer, followed by India. Harvesting the thick, stiff canes is still done mostly by hand and is very labour intensive. Harvested canes are crushed to extract the juice, which is purified and crystallised into brown sugar. It is further refined to make white sugar. It takes about 10 tonnes of crushed cane to produce 1 tonne of sugar, but there are several useful by-products. The crushed, dried cane stalks, called bagasse, are burned as fuel in the crushing mills, thereby making the sugar-cane industry self-sufficient in energy. The remainder is used to make paper, plastics and animal feed. Another by-product, molasses, is used to make treacle and rum. Brazil is leading the way in converting sugar cane into ethanol, a biofuel alternative to petrol.

VITAL STATISTICS

CLASS: Liliopsida

ORDER: Poales

SPECIES: *Saccharum officinarum*

HABITAT: Areas with strong sunlight and abundant rain

DISTRIBUTION: Tropics and subtropics

KEY FEATURE: Most efficient crop at converting sunlight into sugar

WOOD

TREES HAVE PROVIDED MAN WITH A RICH BOUNTY SINCE THE EARLIEST CIVILISATIONS – for fuel, tools, weapons, building materials and for decoration. In ancient Egypt, the tomb of Tutankhamun, who died around 1335 BC, was loaded with ceremonial furniture and images delicately carved from wood. In Norway wooden stave churches dating back to the 11th century are testimony to the durability of wood. Predating even these are the elaborately designed pagodas found in Japanese and Chinese Buddhist temples, some of which have been dated to the 6th century.

Woodworkers divide wood into two basic types: softwood, which comes from conifers, and hardwood, from broadleaved trees. The terms are somewhat misleading since many softwoods are extremely hard and durable, including yew wood, which is as

STILL STANDING The Borgund stave church is one of the best preserved of Norway's medieval wooden churches. It is thought that the stave timbers were made insect and weather-resistant by stripping the bark from pine trees while they were still standing, so that the resin bled out through the wood before felling.

MUSICAL WOOD Sitka spruce is a favoured wood for the sounding boards of musical instruments, such as violins. The back, ribs, neck and scroll (where the pegs sit) of a violin are made of maple, a fine, light wood with an attractive grain. The pegs are made of ebony, one of the hardest woods.

When a tree trunk (known as round wood) enters a timber yard, the way that it is sawn up depends on its final use. It can be cut into planks and segments, with the aim of getting the maximum good-quality wood from the log. The chippings and leftovers go for use as chipboard or pulp for the paper industry. Planks of wood can be finely sliced, sawed or peeled on a rotating spindle to produce thin sheets of wood. These can be used to make plywood (where several thin sheets of softwood are glued together) or for decorative veneers where the angle of cut is chosen carefully to reveal decorative grain patterns.

dense and hard as oak. Conversely, some of the so-called hardwoods are flimsy: balsa, for example, is an extremely light, fragile wood with about one-third the density of other hardwoods – properties that make it a favoured material for making rotor blades and in model-making.

Different woods have different properties and each is selected for its appearance, strength, durability and flexibility. The hardest, densest wood comes from a South American evergreen tree called *Lignum vitae*. The black, close-grained wood is almost twice as heavy as oak and its high resin content makes it waterproof and resistant to rot. Shagbark hickory, which grows in North America, is strong and impact-resistant so is used for axe handles and golf clubs, while willow has the unique flexibility, strength and hardness required for cricket bats (cricket stumps are made of white ash).

The pattern or 'grain' is created by the way the wood is laid down by the tree as it grows (see page 22). By cutting wood parallel to the trunk, along the grain, the result is long straight lines along the length of the wood; cutting across the trunk gives a concentric-circle effect as the cut is made across the grain. Knots in the grain show where the base of a branch came out from the trunk. This is an area of weakness in something like a wooden plank, because knots shrink faster than the rest of the wood, and can fall out. Yet in some uses, the knots add to the overall decorative appearance of the wood – as in knotty pine, used for panelling, and burl walnut, used as a veneer on fine furniture.

Endangered species

According to the Global Trees Campaign, over 8000 of the world's tree species (10 per cent) are endangered. Many of the tropical hardwoods, including Brazilian rosewood (so-named because freshly cut wood has a scent of roses), mahogany, teak and ebony, fall into that category. Though these woods are grown in managed plantations, illegal logging in wild forests still makes up a large part of the market. According to Greenpeace, 50 per cent of tropical wood sold in Europe has been logged illegally. The Forest Stewardship Council (FSC) was founded in 1993 to promote responsible management of the world's forests.

EUROPEAN WOODS AND THEIR USES

Most timber in Europe comes from sustainably managed sources.

WOOD	TYPE	USES
Ash	Hardwood	A good shock absorber, tool handles
Beech	Hardwood	Furniture, flooring, musical instruments
Cherry	Hardwood	Decorative veneers, musical instruments
Douglas fir	Softwood	Furniture, construction, plywood
Larch	Softwood	Construction
Oak	Hardwood	Construction, furniture, ship-building
Pine	Softwood	Construction, furniture, flooring
Spruce	Softwood	Musical instruments
Walnut	Hardwood	Gun stocks, veneers
Yew	Softwood	Veneers, longbows

MEDICINES

PLANTS CONTAIN ACTIVE SUBSTANCES CALLED PHYTOCHEMICALS, which have long been used in both herbal and conventional medicine to fight and prevent illness. Asprin, one of the most widely used drugs in the world, was among the first to be isolated from plants. Today, aspirin is made from synthetic compounds, but the blueprint for the active component came from willow bark. Traditional herbalists from the ancient Egyptians to Native Americans have known of its usefulness to relieve headaches: simply steep some willow bark in hot water and then drink the liquid.

In 1859 chemists managed to isolate the active component of willow bark, a substance called salicylic acid.

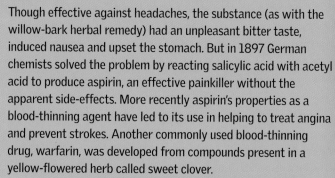

FACTS

EVERY PART OF THE DIGITALIS PLANT, sometimes known as dead man's bells, but best known as foxglove, is poisonous, including the roots and seeds. It was used as a poison in the medieval practice of 'trial by ordeal'.

JUST 5 PER CENT of the world's estimated 300 000 plants have so far been screened for useful phytochemicals.

AN ESTIMATED 40 000 TONNES OF ASPIRIN ARE CONSUMED EACH YEAR.

FACTS

Though effective against headaches, the substance (as with the willow-bark herbal remedy) had an unpleasant bitter taste, induced nausea and upset the stomach. But in 1897 German chemists solved the problem by reacting salicylic acid with acetyl acid to produce aspirin, an effective painkiller without the apparent side-effects. More recently aspirin's properties as a blood-thinning agent have led to its use in helping to treat angina and prevent strokes. Another commonly used blood-thinning drug, warfarin, was developed from compounds present in a yellow-flowered herb called sweet clover.

Two-thirds of cancer drugs have their origins in the phytochemicals found in plants. The rosy periwinkle, for example, contains anti-tumour chemicals vincristine and vinblastine. Another important plant in the fight against cancer is the yew tree. It is the source of paclitaxel, made into the drugs Taxol and Taxotere, which are used to treat ovarian and breast cancer. Hazel trees have also been found to contain this compound.

The anti-malarial drug quinine – now synthesised – was originally extracted from the bark of the South American *Cinchona* tree, while the antiseptic eucalyptol is obtained from eucalyptus trees. Chemicals in the leaves of the poisonous foxglove are used in heart drugs, and atropine, used to treat certain heart conditions and to relax the eye muscles, was originally extracted from another poisonous plant – deadly nightshade.

POWERFUL MEDICINE The highly potent painkiller morphine is carried in the milky white sap of the opium poppy (Papaver somniferum, left). The sap also contains codeine. Digitalis, extracted from the dried leaves of the foxglove (right), has been used in the treatment of heart conditions since its discovery in the 18th century.

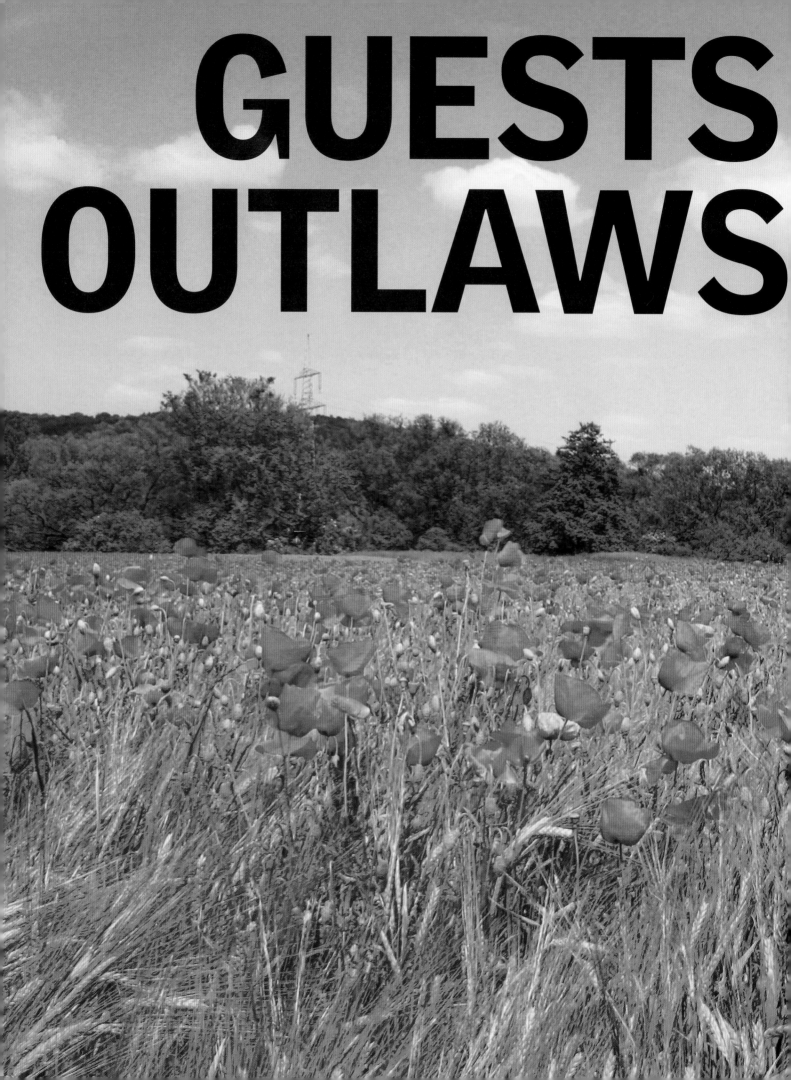

AND

8

EVER SINCE OUR ANCESTORS BEGAN CULTIVATING PLANTS FOR FOOD, humans have attempted to tame nature. Using selective breeding, we have encouraged particular traits in crop plants and developed thousands of novel and attractive ornamentals to enjoy in gardens. An endless succession of plants, sought after for their pleasing colours, shapes and fragrances, have been transplanted around the world, from roses, which have a long breeding history, to tropical orchids, which are now available in supermarkets thanks to modern tissue-culture techniques. Yet for all our advances in breeding and propagation, our control over nature is limited. Weeds such as poppies still plague our crops and gardens. Mostly these unwanted plants are just a nuisance, but some aggressive species pose a potentially catastrophic ecological threat.

NATURE TAMED

OUR LOVE OF GARDENS GOES BACK TO ANTIQUITY. One of the earliest examples were the fabled Hanging Gardens of Babylon, built in about 600 BC in what is now Iraq. Created by King Nebuchadnezzar II to please his wife, who was homesick for the more luxuriant landscape of her native land, the gardens were said to consist of a series of terraces cut into a hillside and filled with water features, walkways, mature trees and lush greenery. Plants taken from their natural environment were able to thrive with the help of irrigation and soil cultivation. Although scholars now dispute the existence of the gardens of Babylon, the terraces still symbolise the fundamental purpose of a garden: the taming of nature.

The ornamental garden, which reached its first high point in ancient Persia, was introduced to Europe by the Romans, who laid out enclosed areas – usually square or rectangular – with roses, vines, rosemary and other herbs, evergreen shrubs, trees such as bay and cypress, and perhaps box and laurel clipped into shapes. Formal in design, these gardens had beds divided by paths and were ornamented with sculptures and fountains. The formal garden re-emerged in Renaissance Europe, when gardeners used borders of box, thyme or santolina to create intricate geometric designs. Knot gardens, in which flowers, low hedges and coloured gravels were laid out to create a complex knot pattern, were popular, as were designs based on letters and coats-of-arms. A knot garden still exists at Hampton Court Palace, near London, whose grounds also house a yew maze – a popular feature of Elizabethan gardens.

In the 16th century, European explorers began returning from far-off continents with exotic plants, and the increased choice sparked a surge of interest in gardening. A number of now-familiar garden plants arrived at this time, among them lupins, golden rod, Michaelmas daisies and phlox from North America, apricots from China, hyacinths and other bulbs from Turkey, and passionflower from Central America.

In the 18th century, English landowners turned away from formal plantings towards a more 'natural' look created by opening up a garden to the surrounding landscape, which in some cases was completely redesigned. Extensive lawns, carefully placed drifts of shrubs and trees, and specially created lakes were used to produce a series of balanced, sweeping views. Among the chief exponents of this style was Lancelot 'Capability' Brown, who wanted to improve on nature while creating a natural effect. His portfolio included the gardens of Blenheim Palace, Oxfordshire.

By this time, the concept of the garden as a reflection of nature had been embedded in Japanese culture for about 700 years. Using sand, rocks, artificial hills, carefully placed plants and flowing water, Japanese gardeners created a natural scene in miniature. The more abstract Zen garden, known to the Japanese as 'dry mountain stream' (*karesansui*), emerged in the 14th century. Containing very few plants, Zen gardens consist of precisely positioned rocks surrounded by carefully raked sand or gravel. The Mughals, Islamic rulers in India from the 16th century, had a tradition of

ROOM TO GROW At Sissinghurst Castle Garden in Kent, the walls and hedges that divide the garden into intimate 'rooms' also provide shelter from the wind, helping to create a series of microclimates in which a wide variety of plants can thrive.

building formal gardens around important tombs. Many of these followed the *chahar bagh*, a Persian term meaning 'quartered garden', as seen at the Taj Mahal, the mausoleum built in the 1600s by Shah Jahan in memory of his favourite wife. Divided into four planted sections by intersecting waterways that correspond to the rivers of Eden, *chahar bagh* gardens were attempts at re-creating the Islamic heaven on Earth.

Towards the modern garden

Formal plantings made a comeback in Europe in the 19th century as exotic plants continued to arrive from overseas. Some tropical types would only grow in the British summer and were 'bedded out' from conservatories and glasshouses – themselves 19th-century innovations – after the spring frosts. During the Victorian era, showy beds of plants such as pelargoniums, verbenas and calceolarias were popular not only in large private

gardens and public parks but also in suburbia as gardening's appeal widened. The invention of the lawn mower in 1830 brought the 'perfect lawn' within the reach of suburban gardeners.

During the 20th century, gardeners began to mix formal and informal plantings, a trend strikingly demonstrated at Sissinghurst Castle Garden in Kent. Created by Vita Sackville-West and her husband Harold Nicolson in the 1930s, the garden takes a sympathetic attitude towards the 'taming of nature'. Although it is divided into sections by formal hedges, the plants within each section are allowed space, spilling over pathways in an abundance of foliage and vibrant colour.

Today, we retain the legacy of history's garden fashions, and the battle to tame nature goes on. Every year gardeners prune shrubs to their allotted space, cut back climbers before they take over, and remove and replenish bedding plants – and then there is the eternal struggle against weeds.

TULIP MANIA The tulip's enduring popularity has led to large-scale production, while hybridisation coupled with the plant's natural inclination towards colour variation have produced around 3000 varieties.

COLOUR CHOICE Azaleas are natives of mountainous areas – seen here in full bloom in the shadow of Mount Fuji, Japan. Since they became popular as garden shrubs in the 19th century, 10 000 cultivars have been bred, in every colour except true blue.

PLANT BREEDING

FOR THE PAST 10 000 YEARS, GROWERS HAVE BEEN SELECTIVELY BREEDING PLANTS in order to encourage particular characteristics, such as good seed size and retention, large flowers and consistency in the size and colour of fruit, that improve a plant's usefulness as a crop or ornamental species. The first farmers would have repeatedly selected the following year's seed from plants with the most desirable traits, such as wheat plants with the largest heads and grains. Over generations, this selective pressure set plants on their way to becoming the crops we know today. Yet there is more to plant breeding than simply selecting the best seed. A pea plant that produced large peas might be crossed with another that had resistance to disease to create a new strain that was both disease-resistant and produced large peas – a process known as hybridisation.

Breeders normally carry out hybridisation in enclosed greenhouses. First, they remove a flower's petals and run a clean brush over its exposed anthers to pick up pollen. In another greenhouse, they remove the petals and anthers from a flower on a different plant, then brush pollen from the first plant onto the stigmas of the second. Once the hybrid seeds have developed, the breeder plants them and waits to see what kind of new plant has been created. Although hybridisation results in plants with desirable traits, it also produces specimens with unwanted characteristics, so breeders follow up a cross by raising several generations, discarding undesirable plants and selecting favourable ones until the new variety breeds true. They then propagate it by taking cuttings and grafts or by cloning – cheaper ways of producing large quantities of a variety than by raising seed, and all result in plants that have the same characteristics.

Tulip fever

The breeding of rare and attractive varieties has started many gardening crazes. When Carolus Clusius imported a shipment of tulip bulbs into the Netherlands from Asia in 1587, people fell in love with the easy-to-grow plants and their brightly coloured flowers. Growers began hybridising the different species, and double-flowered, fringed and striped varieties appeared, but in an apparently random way. The most sought-after tulips had streaks and flames of mottled or broken colour on the petals, and these bulbs fetched vast sums. In February 1637, a single bulb of the variety 'Admiral van Enkhuijsen' sold for 5400 guilders – more than the price of a house at the time. What the growers did not know was that the broken colours were caused not by hybridisation, but by a virus that blocked colour formation. The streaky colours that were responsible for the exhorbitant prices were the one trait that the growers could not control.

ROSES

ROSES HAVE LONG BEEN GARDEN FAVOURITES FOR THEIR COLOURFUL AND OFTEN FRAGRANT FLOWERS. Yet the varieties we enjoy today, with their large, lush heads in jewel-like shades of yellow, red and pink, are quite unlike their simple, five-petalled wild relatives. One hundred or so wild species are found throughout the northern temperate regions, most of them originating in Asia. Our garden roses are the result of thousands of years of natural and artificial breeding between them.

The Egyptians, Greeks and Romans had rose gardens. In those early days, new hybrids would have arisen naturally through the cross-pollination of two species growing alongside one another. New varieties may also have arisen through spontaneous mutation – chance alterations in a rose's DNA – producing unusual flowers that were admired and nurtured.

By the Middle Ages gardeners were deliberately crossing roses to create new cultivars. Several major groups existed in Europe, among them the gallicas, damasks and albas. Gallica roses descend from *Rosa gallica*, a pinkish-crimson 'red' rose native to central Europe and the Middle East. The oldest variety is *R. gallica* var. *officinalis*, known as the Apothecary's rose because its petals were used to make syrups for medicinal use; it was also the emblem of the Lancastrian faction in the 15th-century struggle for the throne of England known as the War of

the Roses. The damask roses, most of which are pink, are famed for their fragrance, the Summer Damask (*R.* x *damascena*) having been prized since Roman times for use in perfumes. The albas are the white roses (although many are shades of pink) and derive from *R.* x *alba*, an ancient European hybrid that may be the result of a cross between *R.* x *damascena* and the wild dog rose, *R. canina*.

East meets West

Rose cultivation received a boost in the early 19th century when cultivars, including some true bright red varieties, were brought to Europe from China. Now breeders could cross hardy European roses with oriental repeat-flowering cultivars, founding the Portland, Bourbon and Noisette groups, as well as the hybrid perpetuals, which when crossed with Chinese tea roses produced the hybrid tea group. 'La France', the first hybrid tea, appeared in 1867 and is often taken as the starting point for modern roses. Meanwhile, rich yellow and orange blooms were produced by crossing hybrid perpetuals with China's pale yellow *R. foetida*.

Further rose groups were created during the 20th century, including the floribundas, with clusters of flowers in a long-lasting display, and the grandifloras, with their smaller but more abundant blooms. But the holy grail of the rose world – a true blue flower – remained out of reach since roses do not have the gene needed to make the blue pigment delphinidin. Then, in 2004, biotechnologists finally hit the jackpot by implanting in rose cells the gene that creates blue pigments in pansies.

With all the emphasis on creating new and beautiful flowers, many highly bred roses can no longer produce strong roots, so breeders now usually 'bud-graft' new varieties onto a vigorous rootstock. Taking a single bud from the new variety, the breeder inserts it into a T-shaped slit cut in the bark of the rootstock (often *R. laxa*, *R. canina* or *R. multiflora*) and binds the two together.

LONG HISTORY Thousands of years of breeding have turned wild rose species such as the dog rose, above, into the 13 000 cultivated rose varieties we enjoy today, culminating in the blue rose produced through genetic engineering.

HOTHOUSE FLOWERS Taiwan is a world leader in orchid production, with total orchid exports worth around £33 million a year. Roughly half of the world's butterfly orchids are bred there.

Orchids readily cross-pollinate, and at least 100 000 hybrid types are thought to exist, with more being created every year through both natural and artificial means.

ORCHIDS

THE ORCHIDS ARE THE LARGEST FAMILY OF FLOWERING PLANTS, NUMBERING MORE THAN 25 000 SPECIES. Although orchids are distributed all over the world, with hundreds of species native to Europe, the tropical types, with their exotic flowers and alluring perfume, have always been the most sought after. Orchids readily cross-pollinate, and at least 100 000 hybrid types are thought to exist, with more being created every year through both natural and artificial means.

The British became enchanted with orchids in the early 19th century, when tropical-plant enthusiast William Cattley grew one from some leaves he found in packing material in a crate from Brazil. The large and sumptuous lavender-coloured flowers that emerged were unlike anything anyone had seen. *Cattleya labiata*, as the orchid was named, whetted the appetites of naturalists of the time, who set out to find more, bringing home huge shipments of orchids from the tropics. Many of these plants died in transit, which only served to make the survivors rarer and even more valuable. Some of the orchids brought back to the UK remained the only known specimens of their type for several decades. Among the most prized of the imports were the slipper orchids, whose colourful flowers resembled a lady's shoe.

If the task of keeping the plants alive in a less-than-tropical climate was a challenge for orchid-keepers, breeding from them was so difficult that for many years people thought orchid seeds were naturally sterile. Then, in 1899, botanists discovered that orchid seeds could germinate only in the company of the correct soil-borne fungus (see pages 62-63).

At first, breeders tried to introduce the fungus during cultivation, but had little success. In the 1920s, chemists developed an artificial, antiseptic sowing medium, comprising sugars, hormones and nutrients in a sterile agar jelly, which gave orchid seeds everything that their fungal partner would normally provide in the wild. Many types of hybrid orchid could then be grown.

Orchid cloning

Perhaps the greatest advance in orchid breeding came in the 1960s, when French botanist Dr Georges Morel developed the tissue-culture techniques that have enabled the cloning of orchids on a large scale. A few millimetres of tissue from an orchid's growing point is placed in a nutrient-rich solution containing growth hormones. The cells rapidly grow and divide, and soon embryo plants emerge that can be separated out and left to grow further in solution. In this way, thousands of genetically identical orchids can be generated from one individual. Orchid-breeding has become so easy that you can now buy orchids at a supermarket.

As years of selective breeding have made beautiful and rare orchids readily available, it should no longer be necessary to take them from the wild, but some collectors will pay large sums for rare wild plants, fuelling a damaging trade. In 2002, rare Peruvian orchids smuggled into the US were reported to have sold for £10 000 each, while in 1995, the rare slipper orchid *Paphiopedilum delenatii* turned up in a batch of orchids sent from Vietnam to Taiwan for use in Chinese medicine. Not seen in the wild since the 1920s and believed to be extinct, the new-found population was tracked down, pulled from the ground and put on the market, pushing it close to extinction again. Today, all orchids are protected under the Convention on International Trade in Endangered Species (CITES), but while buyers remain, the illegal trade will continue.

ANY PLANT CAN BE CONSIDERED A WEED IF IT GROWS WHERE IT IS NOT WANTED. And farmers and gardeners expend much time and effort in getting rid of intruders and making sure they do not return. In botanical terms these plants – many of which are native wildflowers – are very successful. Often the first to sprout in bare ground, they grow vigorously, survive in the toughest conditions and reproduce quickly, usually faster than neighbouring plants. And that's the problem: weeds steal nutrients and light from cultivated plants so are destined forever to be outlaws.

Before the invention of modern herbicides, weeds were an unwelcome but unavoidable part of the farming landscape. Many were annuals with a life cycle that fitted in well with the farming year, on whose rhythms they came to rely for the dispersal of their seed. Corncockle, for example, grew among cereal crops, producing pretty pink flowers – and subsequent seedpods – at the tips of 1 m tall stems. As the crop was gathered in, so were the corncockle's poisonous black seeds, some of which would

then be sown along with the following year's cereal seeds. The corncockle seeds also imparted a bitter taste to any bread made from the grain. The advent of seed-cleaning machinery in the second half of the 19th century did much to control corncockle. The development of herbicides in the 1940s and a shift from spring to autumn sowing of cereals more or less wiped it out in Britain, along with several other arable weeds, such as the yellow corn marigold and blue cornflower.

Perennial problem

Perhaps an even bigger nuisance than annual weeds are the perennial varieties, such as couch grass, creeping thistle, bindweed and dandelion, which remain alive underground during winter. When the weather mellows in spring they use their energy reserves to send up new shoots, put out leaves and grab the light ahead of their neighbours. Many of them also spread widely and aggressively by means of underground stems (rhizomes) or by producing masses of seeds. Rosebay willowherb, which often forms large clumps, uses both methods, creeping via

WEEDS

SPEEDING VINE Kudzu, a climber from Japan, grows very rapidly – up to 30 cm a day. It has become a particular menace in the USA, where it currently infests around 3 million hectares.

FRIEND OR FOE? Although it is considered a weed by gardeners, rosebay willowherb in the wild is among the first plants to colonise an area after fire, helping to regenerate the land.

rhizomes and setting enormous quantities of fluffy seeds that drift off on the wind to settle on new ground.

Alien invaders

Many of the world's worst weeds are 'aliens' that have been transported from their natural home to a new environment. Sometimes the plants arrive accidentally – as fragments or seeds in packing materials, for instance – but often they have been introduced deliberately as ornamentals for the garden or greenhouse. Once they have escaped, these aliens cause havoc, outcompeting native plants for space, light and nutrients. Threatened by few diseases or natural predators, they quickly run out of control and can alter the dynamics of an ecosystem, affecting all the wildlife associated with it.

At the Philadelphia Centennial Exposition in 1876, the Japanese exhibited the kudzu vine, a climbing semi-woody perennial. Fond of its fragrant blooms and large leaves, Americans began growing the vine as an ornamental, while in the 'dust bowl' years of the 1930s its cultivation as a forage crop was encouraged to help reduce soil erosion. However, the kudzu can grow 20 m in a season, smothering everything in its path with a blanket of leaves and even hauling down whole trees with the weight of its foliage. It spreads by runners and rhizomes, and its roots, which can be 10 cm thick and 2 m long, can sprout as many as 30 vines from a single crown. The kudzu can also root at the nodes along its vines, sending up yet more new plants. To get rid of it, every last trace of the kudzu's root system must be eradicated. By 1953, the US government had recognised the kudzu as

EASTERN INVADER Japanese knotweed arrived in the UK in 1825 and now only the Orkney Isles remain free of it.

EUROPE'S ALIEN INVADERS	
According to DAISIE (Delivering Alien Invasive Species Inventories for Europe), more than 6000 plant species are classified as alien in some part of Europe. Below are six of the worst, in addition to those mentioned in the text.	
NAME	**ORIGIN/EFFECT**
Bermuda buttercup	S. Africa/poisonous to livestock
Common ragweed	N. America/cause of hayfever
Giant hogweed	W. Asia/phytotoxic sap
Hottentot fig	S. Africa/outcompetes native spp
Pampas grass	S. America/nuisance on dunes
Rhododendron	M. East/shades out forest floor

a pest and removed it from the list of permissible cover plants, but it remains a troublesome weed in the south-eastern USA.

Another Japanese invader is on the rampage throughout northern and central Europe, North America, Australia and New Zealand. Listed by the Global Invasive Species Programme as one of the world's worst invasive weeds, the Japanese knotweed owes its spread largely to its earlier popularity as a garden plant. With arching, bamboo-like stems, heart-shaped leaves and clusters of creamy white flowers, it reaches a height of 3 m in just one year, shading out other plants. Knotweed also spreads underground via its extensive rhizome system, which travels up to 7 m from the plant and can be 3 m deep. What makes this weed so hard to control is its ability to generate a new plant from a fragment of tissue smaller than a pea. Because of this, the UK's Environment Agency strictly controls the removal of Japanese knotweed. Any plant matter cut down or rhizomes dug up must be collected and disposed of carefully and vehicles coming to and from the site treated to make sure they are not carrying fragments.

Invasion of the waterways

Himalayan balsam is perhaps the UK's prettiest invader, with red, juicy stems, lush, green serrated leaves and delicate pink flowers, but it thrives at the expense of native plants. Imported as a greenhouse ornamental in the 19th century, it escaped and is now common along riverbanks throughout the country. An annual, it produces seedpods that explode when ripe, scattering seeds in all directions and up to 10 m from the parent; some also travel downstream by water.

The sheer quantity of seed set, coupled with its readiness to germinate, results in dense stands of Himalayan balsam that return year after year. Where these stands have crowded out native perennial plant communities, the riverbanks are left bare in the winter when the plant dies back, leading to erosion. Eradication of Himalayan balsam focuses on preventing flowering by either cutting back with a scythe in June or using glyphosate in spring during active growth.

WATER HYACINTH

ONCE A FAVOURITE ORNAMENTAL FOR PONDS, THE WATER HYACINTH NOW HAS THE REPUTATION OF BEING THE WORLD'S MOST DESTRUCTIVE AQUATIC WEED.

The plant originated in the Amazon basin, but now rampages through every tropical and subtropical region, choking waterways with its waxy leaves. A phenomenally fast growth rate enables it to double in size in just 12 days, forming 2 m thick mats of floating foliage that block out light and steal oxygen from the water, suffocating all life below.

As well as damaging the wildlife of lakes, rivers and canals, water hyacinth causes economic damage by clogging up hydro schemes, irrigation channels and fisheries. It infests paddy fields, and does particularly well in nutrient-rich water, which often occurs where fertilisers run off from farmland. According to the World Conservation Union, water hyacinth is now found in 50 countries. The only reason it does not thrive in Europe is because the climate is too cool.

Water hyacinth spreads along waterways as foliage breaks off, and it can be carried into new areas on the undersides of boats. The plant also disperses by means of water-borne seeds, which can survive for up to 15 years. Management of the weed is a constant headache – it grows faster than it can be cleared mechanically, while the use of herbicides endangers other wildlife. The solution may lie in a biological control agent of some kind. Several candidates are being investigated, including weevils, moths, mites and a fungus.

VITAL STATISTICS

CLASS: Liliopsida
ORDER: Commelinales
SPECIES: *Eichhornia crassipes*
HABITAT: Freshwater lakes, marshes and slow-flowing waterways
DISTRIBUTION: Throughout the tropics
KEY FEATURE: One of the world's fastest-growing plants

INDEX

PICTURE CREDITS

NATURE'S MIGHTY POWERS: THE POWER OF PLANTS was published by The Reader's Digest Association Ltd, London. It was created and produced for Reader's Digest by Toucan Books Ltd, London.

The Reader's Digest Association Ltd,
11 Westferry Circus,
Canary Wharf,
London E14 4HE
www.readersdigest.co.uk

First edition copyright © 2009

Written by
Celia Coyne

FOR TOUCAN BOOKS
Editors Jane Chapman, Helen Douglas-Cooper, Andrew Kerr-Jarrett
Designers Bradbury & Williams
Picture researchers Wendy Palmer, Sharon Southren, Mia Stewart-Wilson, Christine Vincent
Proofreader Marion Dent
Indexer Michael Dent

FOR READER'S DIGEST
Project editor Christine Noble
Art editor Julie Bennett
Pre-press account manager Dean Russell
Product production manager Claudette Bramble
Production controller Katherine Bunn

READER'S DIGEST, GENERAL BOOKS
Editorial director Julian Browne
Art director Anne-Marie Bulat

Colour origination Colour Systems Ltd, London
Printed and bound in China

We are committed to both the quality of our products and the service we provide to our customers. We value your comments, so please feel free to contact us on 08705 113366 or via our website at **www.readersdigest.co.uk**

If you have any comments or suggestions about the content of our books, you can email us at **gbeditorial@readersdigest.co.uk**

CONCEPT CODE: UK0138/G/S
BOOK CODE: 636-012 UP0000-1
ISBN: 978-0-276-44329-9
ORACLE CODE: 356500012H.00.24